REAL SNACKS

REAL SNACKS

make your favorite childhood treats without all the junk

LARA FERRONI

SASQUATCH BOOKS
SEATTLE

Printed in China

Published by Sasquatch Books
17 16 15 14 13 12   9 8 7 6 5 4 3 2 1

Cover and interior photographs: Lara Ferroni
Cover and interior design: Anna Goldstein

Library of Congress Cataloging-in-Publication
Data is available.

ISBN-13: 978-1-57061-788-1

Sasquatch Books
1904 Third Avenue, Suite 710
Seattle, WA 98101
(206) 467-4300
www.sasquatchbooks.com
custserv@sasquatchbooks.com

CONTENTS

RECIPE LIST

real sweet

real salty

appendix: the real snacks pantry

ACKNOWLEDGEMENTS

thanks to my mom for teaching me good sense when it came to eating. Junk food snacks may have been mostly reserved for road trips, but they were never such a taboo as to make them irresistible. Wish I could have shared some of these recipes with her.

Thanks to my recipe testers for making sure that what was in my brain made it to the page and for sharing your honest feedback.

Thanks to Kim Boyce, owner of BAKESHOP in Portland, Oregon, for inspiring me to delve deeper into whole grains with her gorgeously written cookbook, *Good to the Grain*, and with her irresistible figgy scones.

Thanks to Susan, Michelle, Rachelle, Anna, Christy, and the gang at Sasquatch for helping me turn this wacky idea into a beautiful book!

INTRODUCTION

the supermarket aisles are full of foods that I love, much of them convenience "junk foods" packed with equal parts favorite childhood memories and industrial additives. The nostalgia of these foods gives me cravings that are often far stronger than I can resist. Who hasn't had a jonesing for a handful of cheesy Goldfish crackers or gotten just a little bit giddy at opening a package of chocolatey Ding Dongs? Sweet or savory, we all have our favorite snack foods.

The guilt sets in when I turn that packaging over and read the laundry list of gums, "ides," and "ates," not to mention added artificial colors and flavorings. Natural food producers have created a whole industry to address this guilt, creating their own versions that are just as convenient, but slightly less processed, than the big-name brands. Unfortunately, these are usually far more expensive than their industrial originals, and, let's face it, not as tasty. Carob is no substitute for chocolate, and lentils do not replace potatoes in a chip, even when the potato has been processed beyond recognition.

It's time to take back our snacks!

This book is all about re-creating favorite childhood snacks, reimagined with more nutritional ingredients (like whole-grain flours and less-processed sugars) that amp up the flavors and textures. These standard pantry items can be found in any grocery with old-world whole grains and other unprocessed ingredients. And for those with gluten sensitivity or who prefer vegan treats, these recipes offer some suggestions for you. The recipes in this book aren't intended to be low-calorie. They are simply *real food* that I think you'll love to indulge in now and then.

REAL INGREDIENTS

baking with only white flour and white granulated sugar is sort of like cooking with only one spice. There is a world of grains and sweeteners with their own flavors and textures just waiting to be incorporated into your baking. Not only will they make your treats more healthful, but they will also make them taste better!

flours

While it's easy to stop at white all-purpose when you think of flour, there are all sorts of flours that each bring a little something extra to snacks. Understanding the flavors and textures of these flours is important when you decide to incorporate them into your cooking.

Flours with Gluten

BARLEY FLOUR

Barley flour brings a slight sweetness to your baked goods, along with a good amount of dietary fiber. Adding a bit in place of wheat flour makes for very tender baked goods, so it's best used for cakes or pastries that benefit from the extra lightness.

GRAHAM FLOUR

Graham flour is a blend of coarsely grown 100 percent whole-wheat flour with all-purpose white flour. You can buy graham flour already blended, or make your own to use as a great general substitute for straight all-purpose flour.

RYE FLOUR

When it comes to rye flour, forget about the strong aroma of rye bread, which comes from the caraway seeds in the dough rather than from the grain. Rye actually has a very subtle wheat-like flavor that is just a bit more complex than traditional whole-wheat flours. It's a great flour to use in chocolate baked goods.

SPELT AND KAMUT FLOURS

Spelt and kamut flours are in the same family as wheat flour, but they have a lower gluten level that is more easily tolerated by people with mild gluten intolerance. Because they still contain gluten, spelt and kamut flours can easily replace wheat flour in most recipes, but they are not recommended for those with celiac or severe gluten allergies.

WHOLE-WHEAT FLOURS

There are many different types of whole-wheat flours suited for different purposes; they all contain the full goodness of the grain. The recipes in this book will often call for white whole-wheat flour (processed the same way as regular whole-wheat flour, but made from hard white spring wheat instead of red wheat), whole-wheat pastry flour (more finely milled, lower protein soft wheat), or traditional whole-wheat flour. You can easily substitute spelt flour (either white or whole-grain) for these flours.

Gluten-Free Flours, Starches, and Meals

It seems like every day new flours show up on the shelves of my local market. While many of the recipes in this book specify particular flours, feel free to experiment. If you have a favorite flour, try substituting a little into the recipes for your own versions of these snacks.

ARROWROOT STARCH

Arrowroot, made from the root of the plant of the same name, is one of the most common substitutes for cornstarch. Arrowroot thickens quickly and can be used in frozen desserts to help keep ice crystals from forming.

BUCKWHEAT FLOUR

Despite the name, buckwheat isn't related to wheat. When leafy buckwheat plants flower, they produce triangularly shaped groats that can be cracked and ground into a nutty flour. Buckwheat flour pairs equally well with sweet or savory foods.

CHESTNUT FLOUR

Although not as readily available as many of the other nut flours, chestnut flour has been used for ages in baking (primarily in Italian baked goods) and has a subtle sweetness, reminiscent of cocoa. It's fantastic when used in small amounts to boost the flavor of doughs, but it's quite dense, so use it sparingly.

CHIA SEED MEAL

Chia seed meal is made by finely grinding whole chia seeds. You can easily make your own with a spice grinder at home. In addition to being high in nutrients, chia meal becomes viscous when wet, and can add elasticity to gluten-free dough, making it easier to handle. Moistened, ground chia seeds are also a very good replacement for eggs in baked goods.

CHICKPEA FLOUR

Chickpea, or garbanzo bean, flour is a strongly flavored flour that loses some of its beany aroma during baking. While chickpea flour has a great texture for baking, it's typically better used for savory baked goods, like flatbreads and crackers, where its flavor enhances rather than detracts from the finished product.

CORN FLOUR AND CORNMEAL

Corn flour is finely ground cornmeal that can be used in baked goods to lighten texture. Because the meal is so finely ground, it doesn't have the grit that stone-ground cornmeal has. Cornmeal is more coarsely ground and is often prepared more as a cereal, such as in grits or polenta. Cornmeal can be white or yellow and comes in a variety of coarsenesses, from stone-ground to fine ground. Added to baked goods, it brings a light crunch and slightly nubby texture.

CORNSTARCH

Cornstarch acts as a thickener, but it also has anticaking properties; it is often used to help keep moisture from creeping into dry goods and forming clumps. When making your own pantry items, it's easy to replace cornstarch with other starches such as arrowroot, potato starch, tapioca starch, or rice starch.

FLAXSEED MEAL

Flaxseed meal is made by finely grinding whole flaxseed. You can easily make your own with a spice grinder at home. In addition to being high in nutrients, flaxseed meal can also act as a binder and, when mixed with a bit of water, is a surprisingly good replacement for eggs in baked goods.

GROUND MILLET

Most gluten-free whole-grain flours have strong underlying flavors, but not ground millet. This fine, powdery flour is hard to distinguish in flavor from its wheat counterpart and is an excellent way to add iron and fiber to lighter, more refined baked goods.

NUT MEAL

Finely ground nuts of any sort—such as almonds, hazelnuts, or walnuts— make a great addition to many baked goods and in some cases can replace other flours altogether. French macarons, for instance, traditionally use finely ground almond meal folded into meringue. Ground nuts bring moisture, flavor, and protein to baked goods.

OAT FLOUR

Oat flour has a soft sweetness that helps create tender doughs. It produces the best results when mixed with other flours; otherwise the doughs can get too dense. I like oat flour best when used in cookie and cracker doughs. Although oat flour can be gluten-free, it's important to be careful of your source, as oat fields and wheat fields are often grown side by side and many oat products may have some wheat accidentally incorporated into them.

POTATO FLOUR AND STARCH

Potato flour absorbs moisture, and while it can impart a lovely flavor and help to bind dough almost as much as gluten does, too much will result in a very rubbery or gummy texture. Potato flour has a strong potato flavor, so it should always be used sparingly. While potato flour is made from whole potatoes, potato starch is made from dehydrated, peeled potatoes. Unlike potato flour, potato starch is neutral in flavor. You can use potato starch in place of cornstarch in most recipes.

RICE FLOUR AND STARCH

Sweet rice starch (like *mochiko*) or glutinous rice starch is a mild starch that is used to lighten baked goods. Brown rice flour can be used as well, but be sure to get it finely ground or your baked goods may have a slightly gritty texture.

SORGHUM FLOUR

Sorghum is a grass grain that is one of the more common flours found in gluten-free baking. Mildly sweet in flavor, sorghum adds dietary fiber, protein, and iron to baked goods. Sorghum needs to be combined with other starches to bake well and should typically only make up 20 percent of the overall flour content.

TAPIOCA STARCH

Tapioca starch (sometimes called tapioca flour) is made from cassava root and is commonly used as a thickener. This starch is also used to make tapioca balls (or pearls). Tapioca starch can absorb up to twice its volume in liquid and can also be used to absorb liquid fats to create a granule or powder, as in Cheese Powder (page 153).

TEFF FLOUR

Teff is a dark, ancient grain that is gluten-free. Teff is most widely known as the grain used in *injera*, an Ethiopian sourdough crâpe. Because of its mild and slightly malty flavor, it's easily incorporated into chocolate baked goods as well as more savory crackers and breads.

MORE FLOURS TO EXPLORE

Flours like *quinoa flour* and *amaranth flour* are packed with nutrition and have a grassy, slightly bitter flavor. *Mesquite flour* is subtly sweet and almost cocoa-like in flavor. A tablespoon of *soy flour* or *kinako flour* helps baked goods stay fresh longer.

GLUTEN-FREE BAKING MIX

You can easily purchase all-purpose gluten-free baking mixes in most grocery stores now, but if you want to make your own, I suggest following the recommendation of Shauna James Ahern (GlutenFreeGirl.com) to combine 40 percent whole-grain flour with 60 percent starch, based on the flavor profile you like. A great combination would be 100 grams sorghum or oat flour, 100 grams ground millet flour, 100 grams sweet rice starch, 100 grams tapioca starch, and 100 grams potato starch (not flour!).

sugars

Hopefully, with these recipes, I'm going to change everything you think about what sugar should look and taste like. Sure, there is a certain visual appeal to a dark chocolate doughnut dusted in bright white powder . . . but have you ever actually tasted powdered sugar straight from the bag? The flavor is almost toxic.

While the sugars and syrups I recommend in this book are still sugar, and therefore not low calorie or particularly good on the teeth, they are more flavorful, a little higher in nutrition, and easier for the body to process than the standard bleached, granulated, or powdered sugars.

Agave Syrup

There has been much debate in recent years as to the actual healthfulness of agave syrup. True, it's just as processed as corn syrup, but I find its clean, bright flavor very pleasing. It does not, however, work as a good replacement for corn syrup in any recipes that require specific temperatures for the sugar.

I like agave best in recipes like ice pops. If using agave syrup in a recipe that calls for dry sugar, you'll need to use two-thirds as much.

Brown Rice Syrup

Brown rice syrup is made by fermenting rice with enzymes to break down the kernel. The syrup has an incredibly buttery sweetness, almost bordering on butterscotch. It works like corn syrup in most recipes (much better than honey or agave do), but has a lower glycemic index. But be aware that most of the sweetness in brown rice syrup comes from maltose, which is a simple sugar that is quickly absorbed into the blood stream, so brown rice syrup can be a problem for diabetics.

Also, because some brown rice syrup is made by using enzymes from barley, those with gluten sensitivities need to read labels carefully to find a syrup that is certified gluten-free.

Cane Sugar

Most granulated sugar is cane sugar, but some is more processed than others. Evaporated cane sugar still has some of the molasses from the original pressing, so it's slightly tan in color rather than pure white. It's easy to use one for one in recipes that call for granulated sugar and is a good choice when making your own Powdered Sugar (page 134).

Coconut Palm and Palm Sugars

Coconut sugar and palm sugar are different, but the names are often used interchangeably. Coconut sugar is a darker, unrefined sugar sold in dry crystal form. Non-coconut palm sugar, also known as date palm sugar, is usually sold in small round blocks. Both sugars are low on the glycemic index and have similar flavor profiles.

Honey

I love using honey for baking, particularly trying different types of honey with flavors and colors that can vary wildly based on what the bees chose to feast on and the time of year the honey was produced. You can substitute honey for up to a third of the sugar called for in most recipes where you think it would improve the flavor, although you may need to cut back on some of the liquid, depending on the recipe.

Muscavado Sugar

Like granulated sugar, muscavado is made from sugarcane, but the molasses is not removed. The darker the muscavado, the higher the molasses content. The sugar is very moist and a bit sticky and can be used easily in place of conventional brown sugar, with much more richness of flavor.

Rapadura

Often sold simply as unrefined and unbleached whole cane sugar, *rapadura* is a whole sugar where the molasses has never been separated from the sugars. It has a powdery texture (unlike raw sugar, which has coarse crystals) and is light tan in color. The flavor is deep and complex, tasting of caramel and molasses. Sucanat (SUgar CAne NATural) is similar in flavor and processing.

Turbinado and Demerara Sugar

Turbinado is a large-crystal raw sugar made from pressed sugar cane juice. Its light golden color comes from a bit of the sugar cane molasses remaining in the crystals. It's best used in preparations that melt the sugar or where the coarse grain adds to the texture. The flavor of turbinado is mild, but slightly deeper than standard granulated sugar. Like brown sugar (which is typically refined cane sugar with a small amount of molasses added later for color and moisture), turbinado isn't much higher in nutrients than refined sugar, but it is deeper in flavor. Demerara sugar is the same as turbinado but comes from a colony in Guyana of the same name.

More Sugars to Explore

Yacon syrup is one of the healthier sweetener choices available, with a strong molasses flavor that works best paired with strong spice or chocolate flavors. *Sorghum syrup* is often used as a sweet topping for pancakes or biscuits, but can also be used in baking in place of molasses or honey. You won't find *tapioca syrup* in your local grocery store, but with a bit of online searching you can find this inverted sugar that can work as a replacement for corn syrup and is great in ice cream.

fats

Butter

Like most people who grew up in the seventies and eighties, I grew up in a margarine household, which was thought to be the healthier choice at the time. Maybe that's why today I have such an appreciation for the flavor of real butter.

Coconut Oil

While coconut oil has had a bad reputation in the past for being high in saturated fats, newer studies have shown that it's actually a very healthy fat. And baking with coconut oil or using it to pop your corn is a dream. The light oil gives a lovely rich crispness. Feel free to substitute coconut oil for the butter in almost any of the recipes in this book . . . except, perhaps, those with "butter" in their name, where the buttery flavor would be missed. Most coconut oils have a very mild flavor, but some (like the 365 Everyday Value brand unrefined coconut oil), have a stronger coconut taste, so you'll want to take that into account when you are choosing your oil.

Flaxseed Oil

Flaxseed oil (also known as linseed oil) may not have the same fiber or antioxidant properties of the seeds themselves, but it's still a great oil full of linolenic acid (an omega-3 fatty acid) and it has a delicious flavor. Always keep flaxseed oil refrigerated, as it is particularly susceptible to spoiling.

Olive Oil

I use olive oil quite liberally in my cooking and usually have two or three different bottles of varying fruitiness and spiciness around. I keep a mild olive oil in a spray can for a quick spritz to "butter" pans. When olive oil is heated, it will lose its more subtle flavors, so there's no need to use your expensive oils in any cooked preparation.

Safflower Oil

Safflower oil is tolerant of high heats and very mild in flavor. It's my preferred oil for frying, as it has a very high smoking point.

TECHNIQUES

many of the recipes in this book rely on a few basic baking methods that are good to know well:

BLENDING THE BUTTER

Blending the butter means working the butter (usually chilled) directly into the dry ingredients to create a coarse, crumbly mixture. This technique is used when you want flaky layers, as you do for some crackers or piecrusts. I typically do this with my fingers, but a food processor or mixer on low can do the work for you.

CREAMING THE BUTTER

Creaming the butter means stirring the butter to soften it and, typically, blending it with sugar to create a light and fluffy base for a batter. As the butter creams, small air bubbles are incorporated; these later help the finished baked goods to be tender. The butter should be about room temperature (65°F to 75°F) to get the best result, and you should always start on a low speed, with either your mixer or food processor, until the butter and sugar are well blended, increasing to a medium speed to finish the fluffing. Creaming is typically used for cookies.

BEATING EGGS OR CREAM

Beating eggs or cream should be done in a mixer or by hand with a whisk. A food processor can't get as much air in as either of these methods.

TEMPERING CHOCOLATE

Tempering chocolate achieves a beautiful, glossy chocolate coating that has a nice crispness to it. Tempering is a way to coax the different fats in the chocolate—all of which have a different melting point—to work together as a cohesive unit. Tempered chocolate not only looks better, but it also sets more easily and doesn't start to melt at room temperature. It is, however, a bit of a pain to do and doesn't have all that much impact on the flavor of your confections. Honestly, unless I need a pretty picture, I tend to skip it altogether.

However, if you'd like to temper your chocolate and don't want to shell out over three hundred dollars for a tempering machine, your microwave and a good thermometer make it pretty quick and easy. Start by chopping your chocolate into small, even chunks. Place 75 percent of them in a microwave-safe bowl. Reserve the remaining 25 percent, which will be added in later.

Heat the chocolate in the microwave at 50 percent power, stopping every 20 seconds to stir the chocolate to help it heat evenly and not scorch. There is nothing sadder than scorched chocolate. You are aiming for a temperature of about 115°F for dark chocolate, 109°F for milk chocolate, or 105°F for white chocolate. This may take from one to four minutes depending on your microwave.

When you've hit the temperature, regardless of whether there are still unmelted chunks of chocolate, stop heating and simply stir the chocolate to melt the remaining solids. Then add the remaining chocolate to the melted chocolate. Keep stirring until the chocolate melts and the temperature of the chocolate is 88°F for dark chocolate and 85°F for milk or white chocolate. Once you've hit this temperature, your chocolate should be tempered.

You can reheat the tempered chocolate if it sets and it should remain tempered as long as you keep the temperature below 90°F. However, if the chocolate gets warmer than that, you'll need to repeat the process from the beginning.

WORKING WITH SUGAR

Some people are afraid of deep-frying. I am afraid of sugar work. There's a bit of magic that happens when sugar reaches different temperatures, and not only is it dangerously hot even when it looks perfectly lickable, but it also requires the strictest attention to prevent the most horrid of burning sugar smells from invading your kitchen. I am easily distracted.

That said, it is satisfying when you finally start to get the feel for all the different thread and ball stages and manage to avoid burning yourself to boot. Your best friend when working with sugar is an accurate candy thermometer. You don't have to spend a lot of money on one, but you do need to trust its accuracy. This is particularly true when working with natural sugars that are more finicky and prone to burning than the highly refined stuff. When a recipe requires sugar to reach a particular temperature, it's best to stick with the recommended sugar and avoid substitutions; alternative sugars may need slight adjustments to their temperature.

And when working with hot sugar, always remember: NEVER LICK THE SPOON!

TOOLS

BAKING SHEETS, PANS, AND MOLDS

There is a lot of baking in this book, but only a few recipes require special pans. Most of my baking is done on quarter sheet pans with one-half-inch rims, which are smaller than typical pans and easily fit two per shelf in a standard oven as well as in the refrigerator.

In addition to sheet pans, it's useful to have muffin tins in both standard and mini sizes. I like the silicone muffin tins, as they clean up more easily than their metal counterparts. A doughnut pan (I like the mini ones) and a canoe-style snack cake pan (to get that true Twinkie shape) are also nice to have.

A few of the recipes also call for cookie cutters. Of course, Cheesy Fish (page 85) are still delicious even if they aren't shaped like fish, but you might make a few more people smile if you pick up the tiny cutter for one dollar.

BENCH SCRAPER

A solid metal bladed bench scraper makes quick work out of cleaning up any sticky rolled-out doughs and also helps lift fragile pastries. This is a six-dollar investment that you'll definitely get your money out of. I like the one by Norpro that also has a ruler on it; it's handy for measuring rolled dough thickness.

BLENDER AND SPICE GRINDER

Quite a few of the recipes in this book require a blender or a spice grinder. There really isn't a good substitute for a well-functioning blender if you want to create your own powdered sugar or cheese powder. You don't have to spend hundreds of dollars; just make sure you get a blender with a glass canister, a metal blade, and at least a 450-watt motor. It will last you for years.

A spice grinder is also nice to have, mostly for grinding smaller amounts than a blender can easily do, but a blender or a food processor will usually work if you don't have one.

DIGITAL SCALE

Want to know the best way to improve your baking? Spend the twenty dollars to get a digital scale. It's amazing how inaccurate volume measurements for flour can be. According to the back of the flour bag, most flour should be between 120 and 130 grams per cup, but most people will scoop a cup that weighs between 140 and 160 grams.

Your scale doesn't have to be fancy, but it should give you gram and ounce measurements, have a tare button to set the current weight to zero, and be accurate to within a few grams. To test your scale's accuracy, weigh one cup of water. It should weigh 8 ounces or about 225 grams.

FOOD DEHYDRATOR

My husband thinks that a food dehydrator falls into the highest level of kitchen-appliance craziness. That didn't stop me from getting one. The fact is, a food dehydrator is an incredibly useful thing to have around for making everything from your own dried herbs and spices to homemade cheese powder, and unlike a lot of kitchen appliances, it isn't easily replicated with tools you already own. Sure, your oven on low will dehydrate, but the higher temperature will cause changes in color and flavor. At a price of around fifty dollars, your biggest problem is going to be where to store your dehydrator (they do take up a lot of space).

If you don't want to buy a food dehydrator, you can still dehydrate food with your oven. With the oven fan on, turn your oven on and off for about five minutes at a time, keeping the temperature between 150°F and 170°F and using an accurate oven thermometer to constantly monitor the temperature. You'll need to do this for several hours.

FOOD PROCESSOR

I went for years without a food processor due to lack of counter space and a basic belief that it was unnecessary. I guess that's the beauty of naïveté: what you don't know, you don't miss. While most of the tasks of a food processor can be replicated in some way with a mixer, a blender, or simply a chef's knife, it's amazing the time and energy you can save. As with a blender, you don't need to spend a lot of money on one; in fact, I think the smaller six- or seven-cup processors actually work best for most applications.

HIGH-TEMPERATURE THERMOMETER

Many of the recipes in this book require precise temperature measurements. Whether you are making a caramel or frying up chips, having a working thermometer that measures up to 400°F is critical for achieving the best results. I have tried all sorts of thermometers from the classic clip-on dial candy thermometer to the spendy instant-read Thermapens. In the end, I tend to rely on a basic Taylor clip-on thermometer that I bought at a restaurant supply store. I do recommend testing your thermometer for accuracy every now and then by sticking it into a glass of ice water and then transferring it to a pot of boiling water. It should quickly come up to temperature and read 212°F.

PARCHMENT AND SILICONE BAKING MATS

Parchment paper is a baker's best friend. Not only does it save hours in clean-up, but it also helps your baked goods bake more evenly. It's also compostable, so you don't have to worry about landfill space. Having a silicone baking mat or two around is even better since they are quick to clean and less wasteful than parchment, but I still find that baked goods brown a bit more evenly on parchment than on silicone.

PORCELAIN SLICER OR MANDOLIN

I have two things to say about these super sharp cutting tools. First, they can be incredibly dangerous (I'm not the only person that I know who has lost a bit of finger). Second, they're irreplaceable in the kitchen. There's simply no faster or better way to get super thin slices of vegetables. Just trust me on this: always, always, always use the finger guard!

STAND MIXER

I think that every kitchen needs a good stand mixer that has at least three different blade attachments: a paddle, a whisk, and a dough hook. Stand mixers make it easier to stream in liquids or sugars slowly without the need of growing a third arm. But you can use a handheld mixer for all of the recipes in this book that call for a stand mixer.

For beaters, avoid those made with a burnished aluminum finish, which will easily tarnish; all that black film will end up in your baked goods. Yuck.

SNACK CAKES

vanilla snack cakes

8 LARGE SNACK CAKES

Despite some tall tales, Hostess Twinkies do not last forever. The box of Twinkies that my friends gave me as a gag gift were, in fact, hard as a rock in less than a year. These cream-filled chiffon cake snacks, made with real, unprocessed dairy and eggs and whole-grain flours, won't last nearly as long as preservative-laden Twinkies, but you will almost certainly gobble them up in no time at all.

¾ cup (90 grams) white spelt or all-purpose flour

¼ cup (30 grams) ground millet or cake flour

1 teaspoon baking powder

½ teaspoon salt

4 egg whites

⅓ cup (66 grams) cane sugar

2 tablespoons honey

¼ cup (2 ounces) water

2 tablespoons safflower oil

4 egg yolks

1 teaspoon vanilla extract

1 batch (about 1 cup) Snack Cake Crème (page 140)

Preheat the oven to 350°F and lightly grease a canoe-style snack cake pan. If you don't have a snack cake pan, you can use 4-ounce loaf pans. Alternatively, create your own molds out of foil by shaping double thicknesses of aluminum foil around a spice bottle and setting the individual foil pieces next to each other in a cake pan.

Sift the spelt flour, ground millet flour, baking powder, and salt together and set aside.

In a dry mixer bowl with dry beaters, beat the egg whites until stiff, about 2 minutes. Transfer the beaten egg whites to a clean bowl and set aside.

In the same mixer bowl, add the sugar, honey, water, oil, egg yolks, and vanilla and beat for 1 minute. Add the flour mixture and beat until smooth, about 2 minutes. Fold in half of the beaten egg whites; once the first half is fully incorporated, fold in the second half.

Pour the batter into the prepared molds, filling them ⅔ of the way full. Bake until golden, 15 to 20 minutes, rotating the pans halfway through baking. Cool the cakes in the pan for at least 20 minutes, then remove to a wire rack and cool completely before filling with the Snack Cake Crème.

To fill the cakes, use a skewer or chopstick to poke 2 holes partially through the snack cake from the bottom, and wiggle around to hollow out some space. Use a piping bag fitted with a Bismarck (#230) tip or a very small star-shaped tip to fill the cake with the Snack Cake Crème.

. . . .

to make raspberry snack cakes, make the snack cakes as directed. Coat each filled snack cake with raspberry jam and dust with shredded coconut. They will be sticky and delicious.

Or for Chocolate-Coated Snack Cakes, try dipping your snack cakes in melted chocolate.

For *gluten-free* Vanilla Snack Cakes, replace the white spelt flour with an equal amount of gluten-free all-purpose baking mix.

vegan vanilla snack cakes

8 LARGE SNACK CAKES

Traditional snack cakes rely on whipped egg whites for their springy lightness. These vegan sponge cakes are still fluffy, but skip the animal ingredients. To make a chocolate version, simply add ½ cup cocoa powder and an additional ¼ teaspoon baking soda to the flour mixture, and an extra 1 tablespoon of water to the wet ingredients.

1 cup (120 grams) white spelt or all-purpose flour

½ cup (60 grams) ground millet or cake flour

2 tablespoons cornstarch or tapioca starch

1 teaspoon baking powder

½ teaspoon baking soda

½ teaspoon salt

1 teaspoon freshly ground chia or flaxseed

2 tablespoons flaxseed oil

¼ cup (2 ounces) hot water

¾ cup (130 grams) cane sugar

1 cup (8 ounces) almond or soy milk

¼ cup (2 ounces) safflower oil

1 teaspoon apple cider vinegar

1½ teaspoons vanilla extract

1 batch (about 1 cup) vegan Snack Cake Crème (page 140)

Preheat the oven to 375°F and lightly grease a canoe-style snack cake pan. If you don't have a snack cake pan, you can use 4-ounce loaf pans. Or, create your own molds out of foil by shaping double thicknesses of aluminum foil around a spice bottle and setting the individual foil pieces next to each other in a cake pan.

Sift the spelt flour, ground millet flour, cornstarch, baking powder, baking soda, and salt together and set aside.

Stir together the chia meal, flaxseed oil, and hot water in the bowl of a mixer. Add the sugar and beat for 1 minute. Stir in the almond milk, oil, vinegar, and vanilla until combined. Add the flour mixture and beat until smooth.

Pour the batter into the prepared molds. Bake until lightly browned around the edges, 22 to 25 minutes, rotating the pans after 15 minutes. Let the cakes cool completely in the pan before removing them.

To fill the cakes, use a skewer or chopstick to poke 2 holes partially through the snack cake from the bottom, and wiggle around to hollow out some space. Use a piping bag fitted with a Bismarck (#230) tip or a very small star-shaped tip to fill the cake with the Snack Cake Crème.

chocolate snack cakes

9 SNACK CAKES

Whether you call them Ring Dings or Ding Dongs, these chocolate snack cakes may just win the award for snack cake with the silliest name. Still, these chocolate hockey pucks are one of my favorite junk food sweets. Adding teff flour to the flour mix increases the complexity of the flavor, making these cakes deserving of a far less silly name.

½ cup (60 grams) white spelt or white whole-wheat flour

¼ cup (30 grams) teff or whole-wheat flour

½ cup (50 grams) cocoa powder

1 teaspoon baking powder

½ teaspoon baking soda

½ teaspoon salt

4 egg whites

⅓ cup (66 grams) coconut or cane sugar

2 tablespoons honey

¼ cup (2 ounces) water

2 tablespoons safflower oil

4 egg yolks

1 teaspoon vanilla extract

1 batch (about 1 cup) Snack Cake Crème (page 140)

8 ounces bittersweet or semi-sweet chocolate, tempered or melted

Preheat the oven to 400°F. Line a 9-by-9-inch cake pan with parchment and set aside.

Sift the white spelt flour, teff flour, cocoa powder, baking powder, baking soda, and salt together and set aside.

In a dry mixer bowl with dry beaters, beat the egg whites until very stiff, about 1 minute. Transfer the beaten egg whites to a clean bowl and set aside.

In the same mixer bowl, add the sugar, honey, water, oil, egg yolks, and vanilla and beat for 1 minute. Add the flour mixture and beat until smooth, about 2 minutes. Fold in half of the beaten egg whites; once the first half is fully incorporated, fold in the second half.

Pour the batter into the prepared pan and bake until the cake springs back slightly when touched and a skewer inserted comes out clean, 10 to 15 minutes. Cool the cake in the pan for 5 minutes before inverting it onto a flat surface and peeling off the parchment. Let the cake cool completely.

With a cookie cutter, cut out 3-inch-diameter rounds. To fill the cakes, use a piping bag fitted with a Bismarck (#230) tip or a very small star-shaped tip to inject each snack cake from the bottom with 3 evenly spaced squirts of Snack Cake Crème.

Place the filled cakes onto baking sheets and freeze for about 15 minutes.

While the cakes are freezing, place a piece of waxed paper onto the counter or a baking sheet. Temper the chocolate, and place it in a bowl next to the waxed paper. Dip each chilled cake into the chocolate to coat and let set on the waxed paper until firm.

For *gluten-free* Chocolate Snack Cakes, replace the white spelt flour with an equal amount of gluten-free all-purpose baking mix.

For *vegan* Chocolate Snack Cakes, see the chocolate version of the Vegan Vanilla Snack Cakes (page 7).

chocolate cupcakes

12 CUPCAKES

While any homemade cupcake is a pretty good cupcake, there's just something about those cream-filled, chocolate-frosted ones from Hostess that makes people happy. These tender, chocolaty cakes are just as delicious, but without the high-fructose corn syrup and partially hydrogenated vegetable oil.

½ cup (60 grams) white spelt or white whole-wheat flour

¼ cup (30 grams) teff or whole-wheat flour

½ cup (50 grams) cocoa powder

1 teaspoon baking powder

½ teaspoon baking soda

½ teaspoon salt

4 egg whites

⅓ cup (66 grams) muscavado or dark brown sugar

2 tablespoons honey

¼ cup water

2 tablespoons safflower oil

4 egg yolks

3 teaspoons vanilla extract, divided

½ cup (4 ounces) heavy cream

1 tablespoon unsalted butter

6 ounces bittersweet chocolate, chopped

Preheat the oven to 350°F. Line a 12-cup muffin tin with baking papers and set aside.

Sift the white spelt flour, teff flour, cocoa powder, baking powder, baking soda, and salt together and set aside.

In a dry mixer bowl with dry beaters, beat the egg whites until very stiff, about 1 to 2 minutes. Transfer the beaten egg whites to a clean bowl and set aside.

In the same mixer bowl fitted with a paddle attachment, add the sugar, honey, water, oil, egg yolks, and 1 teaspoon of the vanilla and beat for 1 minute. Add the flour mixture and beat until smooth, about 2 minutes. Fold in half of the beaten egg whites; once the first half is fully incorporated, fold in the second half.

Fill each muffin cup ⅔ of the way full. Bake until the cake springs back slightly when touched and a skewer inserted comes out clean, about 10 minutes. Allow the cakes to cool in the pan for 5 minutes, then remove to a wire rack and cool completely.

1 batch (about 1 cup) Snack Cake Crème (page 140)

1 batch (about ½ cup) White Icing (page 144)

While the cupcakes are cooling, prepare the frosting. In a heavy pot, heat the heavy cream and butter until the butter melts and the cream is slightly steaming. Remove the pot from the heat and add the chocolate. Do not stir; let the mixture stand for 5 minutes. Then whisk in the remaining 2 teaspoons of vanilla and continue whisking until smooth. Let the frosting cool to room temperature.

Once the cupcakes and frosting have cooled, use a small knife to remove a 1-inch-deep pyramid from the top of each cupcake. Cut the tip off of each pyramid. Fill each cupcake with a dollop of Snack Cake Crème and then replace the tops of the cupcakes. Spread each cupcake with the chocolate frosting. For the classic Hostess look, pipe little loop-de-loops on the top with White Icing.

For gluten-free Chocolate Cupcakes, replace the white spelt flour with an equal amount of gluten-free all-purpose baking mix.

For vegan Chocolate Cupcakes, use the Vegan Chocolate Snack Cakes recipe variation (page 7) and fill as directed. To make vegan chocolate frosting, replace the butter with an equal amount of coconut oil and the cream with an equal amount of coconut milk.

mini cake doughnuts

14 TO 16 MINI DOUGHNUTS

Donettes are tiny little rounds of deliciousness that really don't bear that much resemblance to bakery doughnuts but are somehow still satisfying. You can make your own in a flash with the aid of a mini doughnut pan. While it may seem strange, the addition of rye and barley flours into the batter makes for an exceptionally flavorful treat. To make Chocolate Mini Cake Doughnuts, simply add two tablespoons of cocoa powder to the flour mixture.

½ cup (60 grams) white spelt or all-purpose flour

¼ cup (30 grams) rye flour or whole-wheat flour

¼ cup (30 grams) barley flour or all-purpose flour

1 teaspoon baking powder

⅓ cup (66 grams) cane sugar

Pinch freshly ground nutmeg

½ teaspoon salt

2 tablespoons unsalted butter, melted

⅓ cup milk

1 teaspoon vanilla extract

1 egg

Semisweet chocolate, tempered or melted, or powdered sugar, for coating

Preheat the oven to 400°F and lightly grease a mini doughnut pan.

Sift the white spelt, rye, barley, and baking powder together. Whisk in the sugar, nutmeg, and salt. Set aside.

In a separate bowl, whisk together the melted butter, milk, vanilla, and egg. Add the egg mixture to the flour mixture and stir until just combined. Do not overmix or your doughnuts may be rubbery.

Fill each doughnut cup ½ to ¾ of the way full with the batter. You can do this with a spoon, but I prefer using a piping bag to fill each cup evenly and cleanly. It's important not to overfill or as the doughnuts rise, you'll lose the hole. Bake until the doughnuts spring back when touched, 6 to 10 minutes depending on the size of your doughnut pan. Let cool completely on a wire rack; then dip in melted chocolate or dust with powdered sugar.

For *gluten-free* Mini Cake Doughnuts, replace all the flours with an equal weight of gluten-free all-purpose baking mix.

For *vegan* Mini Cake Doughnuts, replace the butter with an equal amount of coconut oil; the milk with an equal amount of soy or almond milk; and the egg with ¼ cup silken tofu.

one-bite brownies

12 TO 14 MINI BROWNIES

For me, the perfect brownie is equal parts crusty and fudgy. These one-bite brownies, made in a mini muffin tin, fit that bill perfectly.

⅓ cup (45 grams) teff or whole-wheat flour

1 tablespoon cocoa powder

¼ teaspoon baking powder

¼ teaspoon salt

1 tablespoon unsalted butter

1 ounce bittersweet chocolate, chopped

1 teaspoon instant espresso dissolved in 1 teaspoon warm water

1 teaspoon vanilla

⅓ cup (66 grams) muscavado or brown sugar

1 large egg

½ cup (70 grams) toasted nuts, coarsely chopped (optional)

Preheat the oven to 350°F and lightly grease a mini muffin tin.

Sift the teff flour, cocoa powder, baking powder, and salt together and set aside.

Bring a pot of water to a simmer. Place the butter and chocolate in a heatproof bowl over the simmering water and stir to melt. If you prefer, you can melt the chocolate in the microwave; using 50 percent power, heat the butter and chocolate, stopping to stir every 30 seconds, until they are melted. Set aside.

With the mixer on low speed, stir together the espresso, vanilla, and sugar. Add the egg and mix until combined. Stream in the chocolate mixture and mix until combined. Add the flour mixture and beat until smooth and slightly thickened, at least 1 minute. Stir in the nuts, if you are using them.

Spoon the batter into the prepared muffin tin. Bake until just set, 10 to 12 minutes. Set the pan on a wire rack and cool the brownies completely before serving.

These brownies are naturally *gluten-free* if you use the teff flour.

For *vegan* One-Bite Brownies, replace the butter with an equal amount of coconut oil and the egg with ¼ cup of silken tofu.

cinnamon rolls

6 TO 8 ROLLS

These cinnamon rolls are quick to make and far more pleasing than the ones that come in a can. By using a quick bread instead of a yeast dough, you can be eating these tender, cinnamony sweets in less than an hour.

½ cup (60 grams) whole-wheat pastry flour

¾ cup (90 grams) all-purpose flour

2 teaspoons baking powder

¼ teaspoon baking soda

¼ teaspoon salt

½ cup (120 grams) ricotta

¼ cup (2 ounces) buttermilk

1 teaspoon vanilla extract

6 tablespoons (48 grams) muscavado or brown sugar, divided

4 tablespoons (½ stick) unsalted butter, softened, divided

1 scant teaspoon cinnamon

¼ cup pecans, finely chopped (optional)

¼ cup Glaze (optional) (page 144)

Preheat the oven to 350°F. Spray a 9-inch square cake pan with baking spray and set aside.

Sift the whole-wheat pastry flour, all-purpose flour, baking powder, baking soda, and salt together into a small bowl and set aside.

In the bowl of a stand mixer fitted with the paddle attachment, mix the ricotta, buttermilk, vanilla, 2 tablespoons of the sugar, and 2 tablespoons of the butter. Add the flour mixture and stir just until blended.

Turn the dough out onto a lightly floured surface and knead 4 or 5 times to form a smooth dough. If the dough is sticky, knead in a bit more flour. Roll the dough out to a 6-by-8-inch rectangle about ¼ inch thick and brush with 1½ tablespoons of the remaining butter.

Mix the remaining 4 tablespoons of sugar with the cinnamon and pecans, if you are using them. Sprinkle evenly onto the dough, reserving about 1 tablespoon. Starting at a short end, roll the dough into a log and pinch the seam to seal. Trim the ends and slice into 6 even pieces. Place them, cut side up, into the prepared cake pan with their sides just touching.

Brush the tops and sides of each roll with the remaining ½ tablespoon butter. Sprinkle the tops with the reserved sugar mixture. Bake until the edges are golden, 20 to 25 minutes. Cool slightly before serving, and drizzle with Glaze (page 144) if desired.

For gluten-free Cinnamon Rolls, replace the whole-wheat and all-purpose flours with an equal amount of gluten-free all-purpose baking mix.

For vegan Cinnamon Rolls, replace the buttermilk with an equal amount of coconut milk; the ricotta with ⅓ cup soft tofu; and the butter with an equal amount of margarine or coconut oil.

toaster tarts

This recipe, adapted from the one on the King Arthur Flour website, is far more interesting than the slightly stale foil-wrapped tarts we all grew up with. My own personal preference for filling is blueberry, but you can fill these with just about any jam or spreadable filling you like.

⅔ cup (80 grams) whole-wheat pastry flour

⅔ cup (80 grams) all-purpose flour

⅔ cup (80 grams) ground millet or sweet rice flour

1 tablespoon cane sugar

1 teaspoon salt

8 tablespoons (1 stick) unsalted butter, chilled and cut into pieces

8 to 16 tablespoons ice water, divided

1 large egg

8 tablespoons jam or other spreadable filling

¼ cup Glaze (optional) (page 144)

Whisk the whole-wheat pastry flour, all-purpose flour, ground millet flour, sugar, and salt together. Work in the butter with your fingers until there are pecan-sized lumps of butter still visible and the mixture holds together when you squeeze it. Add 3 tablespoons of the water and mix with a fork until it is absorbed. Then add the remaining water, 1 tablespoon at a time, just until a shaggy dough ball forms. You may not need all the water.

Shape the dough into a 4-by-6-inch rectangle, wrap it in plastic wrap, and refrigerate for at least 30 minutes or up to 2 days.

Place the chilled dough on a lightly floured work surface and cut it into 4 equal pieces. Roll each piece into a rectangle about ⅛ inch thick. Trim off the edges to create even rectangles.

Beat the egg with 1 tablespoon water. Brush the egg wash over one piece of the dough. Imagine the dough divided into quarters and place 1 heaping teaspoon of jam in the center of each quarter. Top with another rolled-out piece of dough and press gently to seal around each of the filling pockets. Repeat with the remaining 2 pieces of dough. Reserve the remaining egg wash.

Line a baking sheet with parchment. Carefully cut each dough packet into quarters and use a fork to pinch the edges. Place the tarts on the prepared baking sheet and cover with plastic wrap. Chill in the refrigerator for 30 minutes.

Preheat the oven to 350°F.

Brush the chilled tarts with the remaining egg wash and, using a fork, prick vent holes in the top of each tart. Bake the tarts until they are golden brown, 25 to 30 minutes. Cool slightly before serving, and spread with Glaze (page 144) if desired.

For *gluten-free* Toaster Tarts, replace the whole-wheat pastry and all-purpose flours with an equal amount of gluten-free all-purpose baking mix.

For *vegan* Toaster Tarts, replace the butter with an equal amount of coconut oil. Instead of the egg wash, brush the tarts with non-dairy milk.

animal crackers

Tiny animal cookie cutters are available in many kitchen supply stores or online. If you don't have any, you can still make these subtly sweet, toddler favorites and cut them out into squares or small rounds using the back end of a pastry tip. Or even make them with larger cutters instead of the traditional mini ones.

¾ cup (90 grams) whole-grain spelt or whole-wheat flour

¼ cup (30 grams) all-purpose flour

½ cup (60 grams) oat or cake flour

1 teaspoon baking powder

1 tablespoon cane sugar

¼ teaspoon salt

¼ teaspoon allspice

4 tablespoons (½ stick) unsalted butter, cut into 4 pieces

¼ cup (2 ounces) honey

1 tablespoon milk

1 egg white

1 teaspoon vanilla extract

1 to 2 drops lemon or orange extract

Combine the whole-grain spelt flour, all-purpose flour, oat flour, baking powder, sugar, salt, and allspice in the bowl of a food processor fitted with the dough blade (or a stand mixer with the paddle attachment) and pulse several times to mix thoroughly. Drop in the butter 1 tablespoon at a time and pulse to create a crumbly mixture.

In a small bowl, combine the honey, milk, egg white, vanilla, and lemon extract together. Then, with the food processor running, drizzle in the liquid mixture until the mixture starts to stick together. You may have a little left over.

Line 2 baking sheets with parchment. On a generously floured surface, pull the dough together into a ball. It might be a bit sticky, so flour your hands well. Roll the dough to a little more than ¼ inch thick, being careful to keep the dough from sticking to the counter by turning and brushing with more flour as needed. Using the cookie cutters of your choice, cut out crackers and place them on the prepared baking sheets ½ inch apart. Cover the baking sheets with plastic wrap and chill in the refrigerator for 30 minutes (or in the freezer for 10 minutes).

Preheat the oven to 350°F. Bake the crackers until they are lightly golden at the edges, 10 to 12 minutes, rotating the baking sheets halfway through baking. Remove the crackers from the baking sheets and cool on a wire rack.

For gluten-free Animal Crackers, replace the whole-grain spelt and all-purpose flours with an equal amount of gluten-free all-purpose baking mix. Roll out the dough between two pieces of parchment for easier rolling.

For vegan Animal Crackers, replace the butter with an equal amount of coconut oil; the honey with an equal amount of agave syrup; the egg white with 1 teaspoon freshly ground chia or flaxseed and 3 tablespoons water; and the milk with 1 tablespoon almond milk.

graham crackers

16 TO 18 CRACKERS

Graham crackers get their name from Rev. Sylvester Graham, a Presbyterian minister who developed the digestive biscuits made with a combination of whole-wheat and white flours (now known as graham flour) to suppress what he considered to be "unhealthy urges." The reverend would likely wholly disapprove of this recipe, as these biscuits are hardly bland. Subtle in flavor, perhaps, and packed with whole grains, these cookies bake up crisp so that they hold up to all sorts of decadent fillings and coatings. They're also great on their own.

¼ cup (30 grams) white spelt or all-purpose flour

5 tablespoons unsalted butter, chilled and cut into pieces

¾ cup (90 grams) graham or whole-wheat flour

½ cup (60 grams) barley or brown rice flour

¼ cup (60 grams) turbinado or cane sugar

¼ teaspoon salt

½ teaspoon baking powder

¼ teaspoon baking soda

¼ cup (2 ounces) honey

3 tablespoons milk

1 teaspoon vanilla extract

Place the white spelt flour in the bowl of a stand mixer fitted with the paddle attachment, and add the butter. Mix until smooth, about 2 minutes.

Mix together the graham flour, barley flour, sugar, salt, baking powder, and baking soda and stir into the butter mixture until crumbly, about 1 minute. Scrape down the sides of the bowl, and mix again.

In a small bowl, whisk together the honey, milk, and vanilla. With the mixer on low speed, drizzle the mixture slowly into the bowl of the stand mixer. Mix just until the dough comes together, about 1 minute. It will be sticky.

Pull the dough into a ball, and then divide into 2 pieces. Press each dough ball into a 1-inch-thick disk or rectangle, wrap it in plastic wrap, and refrigerate it for at least 30 minutes, or up to 48 hours.

Line 2 baking sheets with parchment and set aside.

Working with one piece at a time, place the dough onto a well-floured surface. Roll out the dough until it is ⅛ inch thick. Apply additional flour liberally as needed to keep the dough from sticking to the surface or the rolling pin.

Using a toothpick or fork, prick the dough all over. Cut the crackers into 2-by-4-inch rectangles or use a cookie cutter to punch out each one. Place each cracker on the prepared baking sheet, leaving at least ½ inch between crackers. Chill the baking sheet for at least 30 minutes. Repeat with the second half of the dough.

While the dough is chilling, preheat the oven to 350°F. Bake until the crackers are golden brown, 12 to 15 minutes, rotating after 10 minutes. Cool completely on a wire rack.

For gluten-free Graham Crackers, replace the all-purpose and graham flours with an equal amount of gluten-free all-purpose baking mix. Roll out the dough between two pieces of parchment for easier rolling.

For vegan Graham Crackers, replace the butter with an equal amount of coconut oil; the honey with an equal amount of agave syrup; and the milk with 3 tablespoons almond milk.

moon pies

6 TO 8 MOON PIES

My ninth-grade Algebra teacher, Mr. Stevens, had a special way of getting students' attention when they were lazily looking out the window. He'd let the room get quiet and then he would yell, "What are you dreaming about? Moon pies and RC Cola?!!" It quickly became one of my most vivid food memories. A moon pie is basically a s'more: marshmallow crème sandwiched between two graham crackers and dipped in chocolate. Once you've tried one, you'll probably be dreaming about them, too.

½ recipe Graham Crackers (page 29)

1 cup Marshmallow Crème (page 141) or Snack Cake Crème (page 140)

¼ cup Caramel Sauce (page 138) (optional)

6 ounces semisweet chocolate, chopped

Prepare the Graham Crackers, cutting out 3-inch-diameter rounds, and cool completely. Test for crispness. If they aren't very crisp, bake them for a few more minutes and cool again. They need to be quite crisp to hold up to the Marshmallow Crème without getting soggy.

Line a baking sheet with parchment or place a piece of parchment on the counter. Spread one side of half of the grahams with a nice dollop of Marshmallow Crème. Add 1 teaspoon of Caramel Sauce if you wish. Top with the remaining grahams. Give a gentle twist to seal, being careful not to break the grahams. Place the filled grahams on the parchment and let them sit while you make the chocolate coating.

Bring a pot of water to a simmer. Place the chocolate in a heatproof bowl over the simmering water and stir to melt. If you prefer, you can melt the chocolate in the microwave; using 50 percent power, heat the chocolate, stopping to stir every 30 seconds, until it is melted.

Use a spoon to cover the tops and sides of each cookie with melted chocolate. Let the cookies set for at least 1 hour in a cool spot (or the refrigerator) before you touch them or you'll end up with a mighty mess.

For gluten-free Moon Pies, use the gluten-free variation of the Graham Crackers.

For vegan Moon Pies, use the vegan variations of the Graham Crackers, Snack Cake Crème, and Caramel Sauce.

crème-stuffed chocolate cookies

ABOUT 40 COOKIES

There are two types of people in this world: those who eat their Oreos in one piece and those who carefully twist them open to expose their delicious insides, lick them clean, and then dunk the dark chocolate wafers into milk until they are perfectly soggy. Guess which one I am.

Cookies:

½ cup (60 grams) whole-wheat pastry flour

¼ cup (30 grams) teff or whole-wheat flour

⅓ cup (26 grams) cocoa powder

½ cup (100 grams) loosely packed muscavado or cane sugar

Pinch of salt

Pinch of baking soda

6 tablespoons (¾ stick) unsalted butter

1 tablespoon whole milk

1 teaspoon vanilla extract

Filling:

4 tablespoons (½ stick) unsalted butter, plus 2 tablespoons melted

1 teaspoon vanilla extract

Pinch of salt

1 cup (130 grams) powdered sugar

To make the cookies, combine the whole-wheat pastry flour, teff flour, cocoa powder, sugar, salt, and baking soda in the bowl of a food processor fitted with the dough blade (or in the bowl of a stand mixer fitted with the paddle attachment). Pulse several times to mix thoroughly. Drop in the butter 1 tablespoon at a time and pulse to create a crumbly mixture. Then, with the food processor running, drizzle in the milk and vanilla. Mix until the mixture starts to stick together, about 1 minute.

Preheat the oven to 350°F. Line 2 baking sheets with parchment and set aside.

Turn the dough out onto a lightly floured surface. Roll out the dough until it is a little less than ¼ inch thick. Use a 1- to 2-inch round cookie cutter to cut out the cookies (you can reroll any scraps). Place the cookies on the prepared baking sheet. Bake until set, 10 to 12 minutes. Allow the cookies to cool completely on a wire rack before filling.

While the cookies are baking, make the filling. With a hand mixer or in the bowl of a stand mixer fitted with the paddle attachment, cream the butter, vanilla, and salt until smooth, about 1 minute. Gradually add the powdered sugar until fully incorporated.

Spread about 1 teaspoon of filling on half of the cooled cookies. Top with the remaining cookies and gently twist to seal. Let sit for 10 minutes before indulging.

For *gluten-free* Crème-Stuffed Chocolate Cookies, replace the whole-wheat pastry flour with an equal amount of gluten-free all-purpose baking mix. Roll out the dough between two pieces of parchment for easier rolling.

For *vegan* Crème-Stuffed Chocolate Cookies, replace the butter with an equal amount of coconut oil and the milk with an equal amount of almond milk.

vanilla wafers

25 TO 35 COOKIES

To boost the vanilla flavor in these wafers, I stir in the seeds from one half of a vanilla bean. Vanilla beans can vary wildly in intensity and flavor. I look for fair trade, organic vanilla beans that are still moist and highly fragrant, from companies like Amadeus Vanilla Beans (AmadeusVanillaBeans.com).

⅔ cup (75 grams) white spelt or all-purpose flour

¼ cup (30 grams) sweet rice or all-purpose flour

⅓ cup (90 grams) cane sugar

½ teaspoon baking powder

¼ teaspoon kosher salt

1 tablespoon vanilla extract

Seeds from ½ vanilla bean

4 tablespoons unsalted butter, melted

2 egg yolks

Preheat the oven to 350°F. Line 2 baking sheets with parchment and set aside.

Sift the white spelt flour and sweet rice flour together and set aside.

In the bowl of a stand mixer fitted with the whisk attachment, mix the sugar, baking powder, salt, vanilla, and vanilla bean seeds until combined. Add the melted butter and mix to combine. Add the egg yolks and whip until smooth, about 1 minute. Add the flour mixture and mix on low speed just until incorporated. The dough may be a bit stiff.

Scoop or pipe 1-inch rounds onto the prepared baking sheets, leaving at least 1 inch between rounds. For even tops, press down any little peaks that form with a moistened finger.

Bake until lightly golden around the edges, about 10 minutes, rotating the baking sheets halfway through baking. Cool completely on a wire rack. Once cooled, store in a loosely covered container for up to 2 weeks.

For *gluten-free* Vanilla Wafers, replace the white spelt flour with an equal amount of gluten-free all-purpose baking mix.

For *vegan* Vanilla Wafers, replace the butter with an equal amount of coconut oil and the egg yolks with 1 teaspoon freshly ground chia or flaxseed and 3 tablespoons water.

sugar wafers

25 TO 28 SANDWICH COOKIES

How something that so closely resembles Styrofoam can be appealing just goes to show you how mixed up our food desires have become. And yet there is something about the crisp crunch and flavors more of color than of food that I personally can't resist. To make your own, you'll need a special cookie iron called a krumkake iron. A pizzelle maker will also work, but you won't have the same waffle texture on both sides. You can use the krumkake iron to make your own ice cream cones, too.

¾ cup (90 grams) all-purpose flour

1 cup (120 grams) ground millet or cake flour

¼ cup (30 grams) sweet rice flour

2 tablespoons cornstarch

2 tablespoon powdered sugar

Pinch of baking soda

Pinch of salt

1½ cups (12 ounces) water

2 tablespoons safflower oil

Natural food coloring (optional)

1 cup Crème-Stuffed Chocolate Cookie filling (page 35) or Chocolate Hazelnut Spread (page 143) (optional)

Sift the all-purpose flour, ground millet flour, sweet rice flour, cornstarch, powdered sugar, baking soda, and salt together into the bowl of a stand mixer fitted with the paddle attachment.

In a small bowl, mix the water, oil, and a drop or two of food coloring, if using (don't worry that the water and oil won't combine). Then, with the mixer on low speed, slowly add to the flour mixture, mixing until the batter is smooth and pourable, like a thin pancake batter, about 2 minutes. Beat for an additional 2 minutes, cover with plastic wrap, and let stand at room temperature for 10 minutes.

Prepare your cookie iron with a light coating of cooking spray and preheat it. Once the iron is preheated, pour 2 tablespoons of batter onto the iron and follow the manufacturer's directions for cooking. You want your wafers to turn lightly golden brown and be very crisp. If they come out of the iron a bit moist, they will remain limp as they cool. If this happens, place them in a 200°F oven for about 30 minutes or until they firm up. Let the wafers cool completely on a wire rack before using.

For filled wafer cookies, simply spread half the cooled wafers with the filling of your choice. Top with the remaining wafers.

For *gluten-free* Sugar Wafers, replace the all-purpose flour with an equal amount of gluten-free all-purpose baking mix.

These wafers are naturally *vegan*.

peanut butter crème cookies

15 TO 20 SANDWICH COOKIES

Although these peanut butter cookies may not have the traditional Nutter Butter shape, they are just as tasty. For best results, use freshly ground peanut butter. It's easy to make your own at home in a food processor, or you can freshly grind your own in many supermarkets.

8 tablespoons (1 stick) unsalted butter, at room temperature, divided

½ cup (120 grams) unsweetened creamy peanut butter, divided

½ cup (65 grams) powdered sugar

½ cup (60 grams) white spelt or white whole-wheat flour

¼ cup (30 grams) oat flour

½ teaspoon baking powder

¼ teaspoon baking soda

¼ teaspoon salt

2 tablespoons honey

2 tablespoons coconut or cane sugar

1 egg white

½ teaspoon vanilla extract

Line 2 baking sheets with parchment and set aside.

In the bowl of a stand mixer fitted with the paddle attachment, beat 4 tablespoons of the butter, ¼ cup of the peanut butter, and the powdered sugar until smooth, about 1 minute. Transfer the cookie filling to a small bowl and set aside.

Sift the white spelt flour, oat flour, baking powder, baking soda, and salt together and set aside.

In the same mixer bowl, beat the remaining 4 tablespoons butter, the remaining ¼ cup peanut butter, the honey, and the sugar until creamy, about 1 minute. Add the egg white and vanilla and beat on medium-high speed until light, about 2 minutes. Add the flour mixture and mix on low speed until well blended.

Preheat the oven to 350°F.

Fill a cookie press fitted with your choice of cutter disc and chill for 30 minutes or up to 2 hours. Press out cookies onto the prepared baking sheets, leaving at least 1 inch between cookies. If you don't have a cookie press, cover the dough with plastic wrap, chill, and scoop out teaspoon-sized rounds. Flatten each of the rounds with the bottom of a cup.

Bake until golden on the edges, 5 to 10 minutes, rotating the baking sheet halfway through baking. Cool completely on a wire rack before filling.

Spread the reserved cookie filling on the flat sides of half of the cookies and top with the remaining cookies.

For *gluten-free* Peanut Butter Crème Cookies, replace the white spelt flour with an equal amount of gluten-free all-purpose baking mix.

For *vegan* Peanut Butter Crème Cookies, replace the butter with an equal amount of coconut oil; the honey with an equal amount of maple syrup; and the egg white with 1 teaspoon ground chia or flaxseed and 3 tablespoons water.

---

figgy cookies

20 TO 25 COOKIES

My version of the Fig Newton takes its inspiration from Kim Boyce, owner of BAKESHOP in Portland, Oregon. Her lovely, malty buckwheat fig scones look rather outrageous—they resemble purple pastry snail shells—but they are heavenly. So don't be scared when these fig cookies aren't their normal shade of tan; along with the slightly purple tint comes a cookie so tender and jammy, you'll never think of the originals again.

Filling:

10 dried figs, stems removed

½ cup (4 ounces) hot water

¼ cup (2 ounces) honey

¼ teaspoon ground cinnamon

¼ teaspoon ground cardamom

Pinch of salt

1½ tablespoons freshly squeezed lemon juice

¼ cup (2 ounces) port or red wine (optional)

1 tablespoon unsalted butter

Cookies:

1½ cups (190 grams) whole-wheat pastry flour

¾ cup (90 grams) buckwheat flour

¼ cup (50 grams) coconut or cane sugar

Pinch of baking powder

Pinch of salt

continued

To make the filling, in a small saucepan soak the figs in the hot water for 15 minutes. Add the honey and cook the figs over medium-low heat. Bring the mixture to a boil and cook until the syrup is a light caramel color, about 10 minutes. Add the cinnamon, cardamom, salt, lemon juice, and port, if using. Reduce the heat to low and simmer until the figs are softened and the liquid has become thick, about 10 minutes. Remove the pot from the heat and cool to room temperature. When the mixture has cooled completely, transfer it to the bowl of a food processor and puree until smooth. Add the butter and pulse to blend. Store the filling in an airtight container in the refrigerator for up to 1 month.

To make the cookies, sift the whole-wheat pastry flour, buckwheat flour, sugar, baking powder, and salt together into the bowl of a food processor fitted with the dough blade (or into the bowl of a stand mixer fitted with the paddle attachment). Add the butter and pulse until the mixture is crumbly. Then, with the food processor running, slowly stream in

4 tablespoons (½ stick) unsalted butter, chilled and cut into pieces

½ cup (4 ounces) heavy cream

the cream. Turn the dough out onto a lightly floured surface and form it into a ball, wrap in plastic wrap, and refrigerate until the dough is firm, about 30 minutes.

Line 2 baking sheets with parchment and set aside. Lightly flour a piece of parchment. Set the chilled dough onto the parchment, lightly flour, and top with another piece of parchment. Roll the dough out to a 12-by-16-inch rectangle. Then cut the dough into four 12-by-4-inch strips. Spoon the fig filling into the middle of each strip, and then fold the long edges together, pinching to seal. Place the logs onto the prepared baking sheets, cover with plastic wrap, and chill for 30 minutes.

Preheat the oven to 350°F.

Cut each chilled log into 2-inch cookies and place back on the prepared baking sheets, leaving about 1 inch between cookies. Bake until firm and a touch golden, about 10 minutes. Cool on a wire rack before serving.

For *gluten-free* Figgy Cookies, replace the whole-wheat pastry flour with an equal amount of gluten-free all-purpose baking mix.

For *vegan* Figgy Cookies, replace the honey with an equal amount of maple syrup; the butter with an equal amount of coconut oil; and the heavy cream with an equal amount of almond or coconut milk. You can leave out the butter in the figgy filling.

chocolate and orange wafers

16 TO 20 COOKIES

Don't you love it when a mistake turns into something amazing? Rumor has it that Pepperidge Farm's Milano cookies came to be because their predecessor, Naples, got stuck together in transit. Sandwiching two of the chocolate-dipped wafers solved that problem and created an entirely new cookie. I have a particular weakness for the chocolate–orange and chocolate–mint versions. For Chocolate and Mint Wafers (similar to Mint Milanos), replace the orange zest with 2 drops of peppermint oil and the orange juice with milk.

½ cup (60 grams) white whole-wheat flour or all-purpose flour

½ cup (60 grams) white spelt flour or all-purpose flour

½ cup (60 grams) ground millet or cake flour

1 teaspoon baking powder

½ teaspoon kosher salt

8 tablespoons (1 stick) unsalted butter, at room temperature

½ cup (110 grams) powdered sugar, sifted

2 large egg whites

2 teaspoons vanilla extract

¼ cup (2 ounces) orange juice

¼ cup (2 ounces) heavy cream

6 ounces semisweet or milk chocolate, chopped

Zest from 1 orange

Preheat the oven to 350°F.

Sift the white whole-wheat flour, white spelt flour, ground millet flour, baking powder, and salt together and set aside.

In the bowl of a stand mixer fitted with the paddle attachment, cream the butter and powdered sugar together until smooth and creamy, about 2 minutes. Add the egg whites and beat another minute until light. Stir in the vanilla and orange juice. Add the flour mixture and mix on low speed just until incorporated.

Scoop the dough into a piping bag fitted with a medium plain tip (#806) and refrigerate for 5 minutes. Line 2 baking sheets with parchment. Pipe ½-by-2-inch ovals onto the prepared baking sheets, leaving at least 1 inch between cookies (don't skimp on the room between cookies, as they will spread and rise as they bake).

Bake until lightly golden on the edges, about 8 to 12 minutes, rotating the baking sheets halfway through baking. Cool on a wire rack.

While the cookies are baking, make the filling. Heat the cream in a small saucepan over medium heat just until steaming. Remove the pot from the heat and add the chocolate. Whisk until smooth, then stir in the orange zest or peppermint oil.

Spread ½ tablespoon of the filling on the flat side of one cookie and then sandwich with the flat side of another. Repeat with the remaining cookies.

For gluten-free Chocolate and Orange Wafers, replace the white whole-wheat and white spelt flours with an equal amount of gluten-free all-purpose baking mix.

For vegan Chocolate and Orange Wafers, replace the butter with an equal amount of coconut oil; the egg whites with 1 teaspoon freshly ground chia or flaxseed mixed with ¼ cup water; and the heavy cream with an equal amount of coconut cream.

chocolate mint wafers

ABOUT 40 COOKIES

There's one week out of the year when you should absolutely not think about making these homemade chocolaty mint cookies: when the Girl Scouts come around. The rest of the year? Go for it.

Wafers:

¾ cup (90 grams) whole-wheat pastry flour

⅓ cup (26 grams) cocoa powder

½ cup (100 grams) muscavado or brown sugar

Pinch of salt

Pinch of baking soda

6 tablespoons (¾ stick) unsalted butter, cut into pieces

1 to 2 tablespoons whole milk

1 teaspoon vanilla extract

¼ teaspoon peppermint extract

Coating:

16 ounces semisweet chocolate, chopped

6 tablespoons (¾ stick) unsalted butter

1¼ teaspoons peppermint extract

¼ teaspoon salt

To make the cookies, combine the flour, cocoa powder, sugar, salt, and baking soda in the bowl of a food processor fitted with the dough blade (or in the bowl of a stand mixer fitted with the paddle attachment). Pulse several times to mix thoroughly. Drop in the butter 1 tablespoon at a time and pulse to create a crumbly mixture. Then, with the food processor running, drizzle in 1 tablespoon of milk, vanilla, and peppermint. Mix until the mixture starts to stick together, about 1 minute. If the mixture seems too dry, drizzle in the other tablespoon of milk.

Turn the dough out onto a lightly floured surface. Pull the dough together into a ball—it might be a bit sticky, so flour your hands well. Form the dough into a log that is about 1 inch in diameter and wrap it in plastic wrap. Refrigerate the dough for at least 15 minutes, or up to 1 week (if storing for longer than a day, let the dough warm until it is a little pliable before you slice it).

Preheat the oven to 350°F and line 2 baking sheets with parchment. Slice the log into ¼-inch-thick discs. You can slice the discs slightly thinner or thicker if you

wish—thinner cookies will be more crisp and thicker ones will be more firm. Place the cookies about 1 inch apart on a baking sheet and bake for 10 minutes. Allow the cookies to cool completely on a wire rack before coating.

While the cookies are cooling, make the coating. Bring a pot of water to a simmer. Place the chocolate and butter in a heatproof bowl over the simmering water and stir to melt. Once the chocolate is melted, stir in the peppermint extract and salt. Dip each wafer into the melted chocolate and place on waxed paper to set in a cool spot (or in the refrigerator) before eating.

For *gluten-free* Chocolate Mint Wafers, replace the whole-wheat pastry flour with an equal amount of gluten-free all-purpose baking mix.

For *vegan* Chocolate Mint Wafers, replace the butter with an equal amount of coconut oil and the milk with an equal amount of almond, coconut, or rice milk.

cereal bars

These cereal bars are made with my favorite ingredients, but this is one of the most easily customizable recipes you can make. Swap out the nuts, the cereal, the fruit, or the seeds and you have a whole new bar. Feel free to play!

1 cup (150 grams) pecans, crushed

1 cup (100 grams) rolled oats

¼ cup (45 grams) flaxseed

⅓ cup (50 grams) pumpkin seeds

⅔ cup (120 grams) muscavado or brown sugar

½ cup (4 ounces) honey

4 tablespoons (½ stick) unsalted butter

½ teaspoon salt

2 teaspoons vanilla extract

2 cups (50 grams) puffed rice cereal

½ cup (60 grams) dried cranberries

1 batch (about 1 cup) Yogurt Coating (page 146) or 2 cups tempered or melted chocolate (optional)

Preheat the oven to 350°F.

Place the pecans, oats, flaxseed, and pumpkin seeds on a parchment-lined baking sheet and toast until fragrant, 5 to 10 minutes. Transfer the mixture to a large bowl.

In a small saucepan, combine the sugar, honey, butter, and salt and bring to a simmer over medium heat. Continue to simmer until the mixture is melted and slightly thickened, 4 to 5 minutes, remove from heat, and stir in the vanilla. Drizzle the sugar mixture onto the toasted nut mixture. Add the puffed rice cereal and cranberries and stir to coat.

Line a high-sided baking pan with parchment, extending the parchment over the sides of the pan to create handles. Spread the cereal mixture evenly in the pan, cover with a second sheet of parchment or waxed paper, and press down with a second pan or the bottom of a glass to compress. Let the mixture set, still covered with parchment, for about 2 hours.

Lift the set mixture out of the pan by the parchment and place it on a cutting board. Cut into bars. Dip each bar into the Yogurt Coating or melted chocolate, if desired, and let them set on waxed paper before eating.

These bars are naturally gluten-free, if using gluten-free rolled oats.

For vegan Cereal Bars, replace the honey with an equal amount of maple, brown rice, or yacon syrup and the butter with 2 tablespoons coconut oil.

FROZEN TREATS

banana soft serve ice cream

ABOUT 1 PINT ICE CREAM

I first discovered this stunningly simple banana ice cream recipe on my good friend Jen Yu's blog, UseRealButter.com. To get a really creamy mixture, I like to mix in a little bit of thick coconut cream, but feel free to leave it out if you want a stronger banana flavor. You'll need to freeze the bananas overnight, so be sure to plan accordingly.

3 to 4 bananas, peeled and frozen

1 to 2 tablespoons coconut cream

Seeds from 1 vanilla bean or 1 teaspoon vanilla extract

In a blender or food processor, combine the frozen bananas, coconut cream, and vanilla bean seeds. Puree until smooth. Serve immediately or freeze for an hour for a more scoopable texture.

This ice cream is naturally *gluten-free* and *vegan*.

vanilla ice cream

ABOUT 1 PINT ICE CREAM

There's no need to worry about getting the custard right in this egg-free ice cream. A little brown rice sugar helps keep the ice cream from crystallizing and also adds a lovely buttery note—you'll never miss the eggs.

⅓ cup (60 grams) turbinado or cane sugar

1 tablespoon brown rice syrup

½ teaspoon salt

2 cups (16 ounces) heavy cream, divided

1 cup (8 ounces) whole milk

½ teaspoon vanilla extract

1 vanilla bean, split

In a medium saucepan over medium-low heat, combine the sugar, brown rice syrup, salt, and 1 cup of the heavy cream. Cook until the sugar dissolves and the mixture thickens just slightly, about 5 minutes. Stir in the milk, vanilla extract, vanilla bean, and the remaining 1 cup of heavy cream. Transfer the mixture to a covered container and place in the refrigerator to chill for at least 1 hour. Churn according to your ice cream maker's directions, removing the vanilla bean before churning.

This ice cream is naturally gluten-free.

For vegan Vanilla Ice Cream, replace the heavy cream with 1 cup of vanilla soy yogurt (or, if you like the flavor, coconut cream) and the milk with 2 cups of almond milk. You'll also want to stir in 1 teaspoon arrowroot powder to help create a thick, creamy texture. Mix the arrowroot powder with 1 tablespoon of the almond milk and add it along with the rest of the almond milk.

ice cream sandwiches

6 SANDWICHES

The trick to getting package-perfect ice cream sandwiches is to make sure your ice cream is very well frozen, so be sure to allow yourself enough time to freeze your treats before sharing them.

1 batch (1 pint) Banana Soft Serve Ice Cream (page 58) or Vanilla Ice Cream (page 59), freshly churned

1¼ cups (150 grams) white whole-wheat or all-purpose flour

¼ cup (30 grams) chestnut or whole-wheat flour

¼ cup (20 grams) cocoa powder

½ teaspoon baking powder

¼ teaspoon salt

8 tablespoons (1 stick) unsalted butter

½ cup (100 grams) muscavado or brown sugar

1 egg

½ teaspoon vanilla extract

Line a high-sided baking dish with waxed paper, extending the waxed paper over the sides of the dish to create handles. Pour the ice cream into the pan and use a spatula to spread it evenly; it should be about ½ inch thick. Cover with another piece of waxed paper and freeze for at least 1 hour, preferably overnight, until the ice cream is very firm.

While the ice cream is freezing, prepare the sandwich cookie. Sift the white whole-wheat flour, chestnut flour, cocoa powder, baking powder, and salt together and set aside.

In the bowl of a stand mixer fitted with the paddle attachment, cream the butter and sugar together until light and fluffy, about 2 to 3 minutes. Add the egg and vanilla and beat until light, about 2 minutes. Add the flour mixture and mix on medium speed until well blended. Turn the dough out onto a lightly floured surface and form into a ball. Wrap with plastic wrap and chill for 1 hour.

Preheat the oven to 375°F. Line a baking sheet with parchment.

Place the chilled dough onto a generously floured surface and roll it out to a ¼-inch-thick rectangle. Prick the dough all over with a toothpick or fork. With a knife or cookie cutter, cut out into your preferred ice cream sandwich shape. Don't forget to cut out an even number! Place on the prepared baking sheets about 1 inch apart and bake until the cookies start to darken at the edges, 8 to 10 minutes, rotating the baking sheets halfway through baking. Cool completely on a wire rack.

When you are ready to assemble the ice cream sandwiches, remove the ice cream from the baking dish using the waxed paper handles. Remove the top waxed paper. Using a knife or a cookie cutter, cut the ice cream out into the same shape as the cookies. Dip the knife or cookie cutter into warm water between cuts. Place the cut ice cream between 2 cookies and freeze the assembled sandwiches until firm.

For *gluten-free* Ice Cream Sandwiches, replace the white whole-wheat flour with an equal amount of gluten-free all-purpose baking mix. Roll out the dough between two pieces of parchment for easier rolling.

For *vegan* Ice Cream Sandwiches, replace the butter with an equal amount of coconut oil and the egg with 1 teaspoon ground chia or flaxseed mixed with 3 tablespoons water. Use Banana Soft Serve Ice Cream (page 58) or vegan Vanilla Ice Cream (page 59) to fill the sandwiches.

chocolate peanut ice cream cones

5 TO 7 CONES

While the jingle of the ice cream truck evokes a certain excitement, freezer-burned Drumsticks will probably no longer hold the same charm they once did when you've made your own chocolate-dipped, peanut-crusted ice cream cones. You'll need a krumkake iron to make these cones; if you don't have one, you can still create delicious cones following the alternate instructions below.

¼ cup (30 grams) white whole-wheat flour

2 tablespoons ground millet or sweet rice flour

1 egg

¼ cup (50 grams) cane sugar

1 teaspoon vanilla extract

Pinch of salt

2 tablespoons milk

2 tablespoons unsalted butter, melted

12 ounces semisweet chocolate, chopped, divided

1 cup (140 grams) peanuts, crushed

1 batch (about 1 pint) Vanilla Ice Cream (page 59)

Sift the white whole-wheat flour and ground millet flour together and set aside.

In a medium bowl, combine the egg and sugar. Whisk until the color lightens, about 2 minutes. Stir in the vanilla and salt. Add the flour mixture and stir to combine. Add the milk and butter and gently stir just to combine.

Prepare a krumkake iron with a light coating of cooking spray and preheat it. Once the iron is preheated, pour 2 tablespoons of batter onto the iron and follow the manufacturer's directions for cooking. You want your wafers to turn golden brown and be very crisp.

If you don't have a krumkake iron, preheat the oven to 400°F and line 2 baking sheets with parchment. Spread the batter into 4 rounds on each baking sheet, leaving 2 inches between the rounds. Bake until the edges just start to darken, about 5 minutes.

While the rounds are still hot, carefully lift each one with a spatula and shape into a cone. Let the cones cool completely. If the cones are still a bit moist, they will remain

limp after they cool. If this happens, place them in a 200°F oven until they are crisp, about 15 minutes. Allow the cones to cool completely again.

While the cones are cooling, place 6 ounces of the chocolate in a microwave-safe bowl. Using 50 percent power, heat the chocolate in the microwave, stopping to stir every 30 seconds, until it is melted. Spoon 1 tablespoon of the melted chocolate into each cooled cone and turn the cone to lightly coat the inside. Set aside to let the chocolate harden (you can refrigerate the cones to speed the process, but the cones may not be as crisp). They can be stored in an airtight container at this point for a few days.

When you are ready to serve the ice cream cones, melt the remaining 6 ounces of chocolate in the microwave, using 50 percent power and stopping to stir every 30 seconds, until the chocolate is melted. Set the melted chocolate on the counter and place the peanuts in a wide bowl right next to the chocolate.

Working with one cone at a time, top with a scoop of ice cream, pushing the ice cream securely into the cone and leaving a nice, rounded top that overhangs the sides of the cone slightly. Dip the ice cream into the melted chocolate and roll it in the peanuts or sprinkle the peanuts on top. This will get a bit messy, but the results are worth it. Serve immediately.

For gluten-free Chocolate Peanut Ice Cream Cones, replace the white whole-wheat flour with an equal amount of gluten-free all-purpose baking mix.

For vegan Chocolate Peanut Ice Cream Cones, replace the egg with 1 teaspoon ground chia or flaxseed and 3 tablespoons water; the milk with an equal amount of almond or rice milk; and the butter with an equal amount of coconut oil. Use the vegan variation of the Vanilla Ice Cream (page 59).

orange vanilla ice pops

5 TO 7 POPS

These creamy blended citrus pops may taste like dessert, but I think they make a great breakfast smoothie to go. For a decorative tip, add a tablespoon of orange juice to the mold and freeze before filling. To free your ice pops from their molds, wrap the molds in a warm, wet cloth for about 30 seconds and lightly twist the ice pops to loosen.

1 cup freshly squeezed orange juice (about 8 oranges)

1 cup plain yogurt

¼ cup honey

1 teaspoon vanilla extract

In a blender or food processor, combine the orange juice, yogurt, and honey. Blend until the sugar dissolves, about 1 to 2 minutes. Stir in the vanilla. Pour the mixture into push-up or ice pop molds and freeze for at least 4 hours.

These ice pops are naturally gluten-free.

For vegan Orange Vanilla Ice Pops, replace the yogurt with an equal amount of your favorite plain or vanilla non-dairy yogurt and the honey with an equal amount of agave syrup.

chocolate pudding ice pops

5 TO 7 POPS

Apparently, a whole generation is now growing up without knowing the joys of creamy, chocolaty pudding pops. Can you imagine? I hope you do your part and share these with your sons, daughters, nieces, nephews, or neighborhood kids.

¼ cup (50 grams) coconut or cane sugar

2 tablespoons cocoa powder

1½ tablespoons arrowroot powder

¼ teaspoon salt

1 cup (8 ounces) whole milk, divided

1 egg

1 egg yolk

½ teaspoon vanilla extract

Sift the sugar, cocoa powder, arrowroot powder, and salt into a heavy-bottomed pot. Whisk in ¼ cup of the milk to make a smooth paste. Whisk in the egg and egg yolk, followed by the remaining ¾ cup of milk.

Place the pot over low heat and stir constantly with a wooden spoon. The mixture needs to heat very slowly to keep from curdling. Once it starts to thicken, after about 5 to 10 minutes, remove the mixture from the heat immediately. Stir in the vanilla and allow the mixture to cool to room temperature. Spoon into 3-ounce ice pop molds and freeze for at least 4 hours.

. . . .

to make vanilla pudding Ice Pops, simply leave out the cocoa powder and increase the vanilla to 1 teaspoon.

Strawberry Pudding Ice Pops are equally easy: leave out the cocoa powder and add ¼ cup strawberry puree when you add the vanilla.

These ice pops are naturally *gluten-free*.

Although I haven't found a great way of making *vegan* pudding that I love, vegan fudgsicles are a great substitute. While they are less creamy, they are chocolaty delicious. Simply mix 1 cup of almond or coconut milk with ¼ cup coconut or cane sugar, 2 tablespoons cocoa powder, ½ teaspoon vanilla, and a pinch of salt in a heavy-bottomed pot over low heat until the sugar dissolves and the mixture is evenly combined. Cool to room temperature before pouring into the molds and freezing for 4 hours.

CONFECTIONS

caramel corn

ABOUT 8 CUPS

You'll have to add your own prize, but this caramel corn, with the addition of pecans and almonds and a little spice from dried red chile flakes, is far more satisfying than the stale stuff you'll find in the cardboard box.

⅓ cup (80 grams) unpopped popcorn

1 tablespoon coconut oil

⅓ cup peanuts (optional)

⅓ cup pecans (optional)

⅓ cup slivered almonds (optional)

2 tablespoons water

1 cup (200 grams) cane sugar

½ teaspoon salt

1 tablespoon brown rice or golden syrup

1 teaspoon baking soda

Flake salt (optional)

Dried red chile flakes (optional)

Pop the corn in a large, heavy-bottomed pot, or in a popcorn popper, with the coconut oil. Place in a large bowl. The bowl should only be about half full so that you have plenty of room to toss the popcorn to coat.

If you are using the peanuts, pecans, and slivered almonds, toast them lightly in a 350°F oven until fragrant, about 5 minutes, and place them in the bowl with the popcorn.

Line a baking sheet with aluminum foil and set aside.

In a heavy-bottomed pot, bring the water, sugar, salt, and brown rice syrup to a boil over medium-low heat, stirring constantly and using a moistened pastry brush to brush down any errant crystals that form on the side of the pot. Once the sugar is boiling, stop brushing and stir occasionally while bringing the mixture to 310°F. This may take up to 20 minutes, so be patient, keeping the heat on medium-low so that the sugar doesn't burn. Every once in a while, rotate the pot to avoid hot spots. When the sugar reaches 310°F, immediately remove it from the heat and stir the baking soda in briskly.

Pour the caramel over the popcorn and nuts and stir with a spoon to coat. Pour the coated popcorn onto the prepared baking sheet and sprinkle with the flake salt and red chile flakes, if desired. Let the caramel cool and harden before serving.

This caramel corn is naturally *gluten-free* and *vegan*.

chocolate toffee bars

12 TO 15 BARS

Brown rice syrup makes this toffee deliciously buttery. The high heat required for toffee doesn't work very well for sugars that are unrefined like rapidura, so don't be tempted to substitute here. Evaporated cane sugar caramelizes more consistently without scorching. If getting perfect rectangles is important, use a bar-shaped silicone candy mold and pour the hot toffee into it to cool.

8 tablespoons (1 stick) unsalted butter

¾ cup (150 grams) cane sugar

¼ teaspoon salt

1 tablespoon brown rice or golden syrup

¼ cup finely chopped almonds

½ teaspoon vanilla extract

12 ounces milk chocolate, tempered or melted, divided

Butter, or line with a silicone baking mat, a 9-by-13-inch rimmed baking sheet.

In a heavy-bottomed pot, bring the butter, sugar, salt, and brown rice syrup to a boil over medium-low heat, stirring constantly and using a moistened pastry brush to brush down any errant crystals that form on the side of the pot. Once the sugar is boiling, stop brushing and stir occasionally while bringing the mixture to 300°F. This may take up to 20 minutes, so be patient, keeping the heat on medium-low so that the sugar doesn't burn. Every once in a while, rotate the pot to avoid hot spots. When the sugar reaches 300°F, immediately remove it from the heat and stir in the almonds and vanilla.

Pour the toffee mixture into the prepared pan and spread it to an even layer about ¼ inch thick. Let set until firm, about 15 minutes.

After the toffee has set, pour 4 ounces of the tempered chocolate onto the cooled toffee and spread to coat. Place in a cool spot (or the refrigerator) to set, about 30 minutes.

Once the melted chocolate has set on the toffee, remove the toffee from the pan and slice into rectangles (don't worry if some pieces break; they will still taste delicious). Place the bars chocolate side down on a large sheet of waxed paper.

Pour the remaining 8 ounces of tempered chocolate over the toffee and spread to coat, being sure to cover the sides as well. Place in a cool spot (or the refrigerator) to set, about 30 minutes.

These bars are naturally gluten-free.

For vegan Chocolate Toffee Bars, replace the butter with 4 tablespoons coconut oil or margarine plus 2 tablespoons almond milk.

chocolate caramel cookie sticks

10 TO 15 COOKIE STICKS

Is it a cookie? Is it a candy? Well, it's a little of both. Mars calls Twix a "cookie bar." This homemade version may have a few steps, but they keep well, so make a big batch and enjoy them for a while.

1¼ cups (150 grams) white spelt or all-purpose flour

½ cup (60 grams) sweet rice flour

1 teaspoon salt

6 tablespoons (¾ stick) unsalted butter, at room temperature

⅔ cup (75 grams) powdered sugar

1 egg white

1 teaspoon vanilla

⅓ cup (2½ ounces) Caramel Sauce (page 138)

12 ounces semisweet chocolate, tempered or melted

Preheat the oven to 375°F.

Sift the white spelt flour, sweet rice flour, and salt together and set aside.

In the bowl of a stand mixer fitted with the paddle attachment, cream the butter and powdered sugar together until light and fluffy, about 2 minutes. Add the egg white and vanilla and beat until creamy, about 1 minute. Add the flour mixture and mix on low speed just until incorporated. Refrigerate until firm, about 20 minutes.

Line a 9-by-13-inch rimmed baking sheet with parchment, extending the parchment over the sides of the pan to create handles. Roll out the chilled dough until it is a little more than ¼ inch thick. Prick the dough all over with a fork and carefully place the dough onto the prepared baking sheet. Bake until very lightly golden, 15 to 20 minutes, rotating the baking sheet halfway through baking.

Allow the baked shortbread to cool slightly in the pan and then spread the Caramel Sauce thickly over the top.

Remove the caramel-covered shortbread from the pan, using the parchment as handles, and place on a large, stable cutting surface. Using a large, sharp knife, cut the shortbread into ½-by-3-inch bars.

Line a tray with waxed paper. Dip the cookie sticks in the melted chocolate, covering them completely. Place the dipped cookie sticks on the prepared tray. Place in a cool spot (or the refrigerator) to set, about 30 minutes. Uneaten cookie sticks will keep in an airtight container for 2 weeks, or longer in the refrigerator.

For gluten-free Chocolate Caramel Cookie Sticks, replace the white spelt flour with an equal amount of gluten-free all-purpose baking mix.

For vegan Chocolate Caramel Cookie Sticks, replace the butter with an equal amount of coconut oil and the egg white with 1 teaspoon ground chia or flaxseed and 3 tablespoons water.

yogurt-covered raisins

ABOUT 2 CUPS RAISINS

These yogurt-covered raisins are a test in patience and meticulousness. Do you have the will to separate out one hundred individual raisins so that they dry perfectly? Neither do I. Instead, I simply make yogurt raisin clusters that are easy to munch on a handful at a time. Feel free to substitute dried cranberries or nuts for the raisins—the yogurt coating is just as good on them.

2 cups raisins

1 tablespoon powdered sugar

1 batch (about 1 cup) Yogurt Coating (page 146)

Line a baking sheet with parchment or waxed paper and set aside.

In a medium-sized bowl, quickly toss the raisins in the powdered sugar to lightly coat, and then drop them into the yogurt coating. Stir to fully coat each raisin.

Pour the mixture out onto the prepared baking sheet and, using a fork or a chopstick, separate the raisins as much as you wish. Let the raisins sit until the yogurt coating sets, about 30 minutes, then break them apart into clumps.

These coated raisins are naturally *gluten-free* and *vegan* (if using the vegan Yogurt Coating on page 146).

CRACKERS

cheesy fish

80 TO 100 CRACKERS

Tiny cutters work best for replicating the classic cheese fish crackers. You can find them online with a quick search, or make your own from a soda can with a great little tutorial at Miss Anthropist's Kitchen (MissAnthropistsKitchen.com). The corn and oat flours in this recipe boost the nutrition and give a more complex texture to the crackers.

¼ cup (30 grams) all-purpose flour

¼ cup (30 grams) whole-wheat flour

¼ cup (30 grams) corn or all-purpose flour

¼ cup (30 grams) oat or all-purpose flour

¼ teaspoon salt

2 ounces grated, loosely packed mild cheddar cheese

2 tablespoons coconut oil or unsalted butter

2 to 3 tablespoons hot water, divided

Preheat the oven to 350°F. Line 2 baking sheets with parchment and set aside.

Combine the all-purpose flour, whole-wheat flour, corn flour, oat flour, and salt in the bowl of a food processor fitted with the dough blade and pulse to combine. Add the cheese and coconut oil, and pulse to incorporate. Scrape down the sides of the food processor to free any trapped flour. With the food processor running, drizzle in the hot water, a little at a time, just until the mixture begins to pull together. You may not use all of the water.

Turn the dough out onto a lightly floured surface and gather it into a ball. Knead gently once or twice. Roll out the dough until it is slightly less than ⅛ inch thick.

Using a very small fish-shaped cutter, or the cutter of your choice, cut out the crackers and carefully place them on the prepared baking sheets. Bake until golden around the edges, about 10 to 12 minutes, and cool before serving.

For *gluten-free* Cheesy Fish, replace the all-purpose and whole-wheat flours with an equal amount of gluten-free all-purpose baking mix. Roll out the dough between two pieces of parchment for easier rolling.

For *vegan* fish crackers, replace the cheese with 1 teaspoon nutritional yeast and ½ teaspoon onion powder. Add an additional tablespoon of water. Increase the salt to ½ teaspoon.

butter crackers

35 TO 45 CRACKERS

A touch of sugar makes these flaky crackers equally as tasty with peanut butter as they are with cheese. Look for a fluted edge cookie cutter to make your crackers look like the classic Ritz crackers.

⅓ cup (45 grams) white spelt or all-purpose flour

⅔ cup (90 grams) white whole-wheat flour

¼ cup (30 grams) oat or cake flour

1½ teaspoons baking powder

1½ tablespoons cane sugar

½ teaspoon salt

3 tablespoons unsalted butter, chilled and cut into pieces

1 tablespoon flaxseed or olive oil

¼ cup (2 ounces) ice water, divided

1 egg

1 tablespoon milk

2 tablespoons unsalted butter, melted

¼ teaspoon salt

Preheat the oven to 400°F. Line 2 baking sheets with parchment and set aside.

Sift the white spelt flour, white whole-wheat flour, oat flour, baking powder, sugar, and salt together. Pour into the bowl of a food processor fitted with the dough blade (or in the bowl of a stand mixer fitted with the paddle attachment). Add the chilled butter and pulse to create a coarse crumb mixture. With the food processor running, stream in the flaxseed oil, followed by the water, 1 tablespoon at a time, until the mixture starts to form large clumps.

Turn the dough out onto a well-floured surface and gather it into a ball. Knead gently once or twice. Sprinkle a little more flour on top of the dough and roll it out until it is ¼ inch thick, rotating the dough by 90 degrees after each roll.

Prick the dough all over with a fork, making sure it is well pierced. Using a small cookie cutter of your choice, cut out the crackers and carefully place them on the prepared baking sheets.

In a small bowl, lightly whisk the egg with the milk. Using a pastry brush, coat the tops of the crackers with the egg wash.

Bake just until the crackers begin to brown, 5 to 10 minutes.

While the crackers are baking, stir the melted butter and salt together in a small bowl. Brush the mixture onto the freshly baked, still warm crackers before serving.

For gluten-free Butter Crackers, replace the white spelt and white whole-wheat flours with an equal amount of gluten-free all-purpose baking mix. Roll out the dough between two pieces of parchment for easier rolling.

For vegan Butter Crackers, replace the butter with an equal amount of vegan margarine or coconut oil and the egg wash with soy milk.

salty water crackers

ABOUT 70 CRACKERS

Saltines, the modern (and saltier) version of the water biscuit, are the classic soup cracker. Cut this homemade version into little squares for traditional crackers, or into little rounds for "oyster" crackers. I use a pastry wheel to give a scalloped edge to these crackers, but a knife works just as well.

1½ cups (180 grams) white spelt or all-purpose flour

½ cup (60 grams) ground millet or sweet rice flour

1 teaspoon salt

Pinch of baking soda

2 tablespoons coconut oil or unsalted butter

8 tablespoons hot water (approximately 150°F)

Flake salt for sprinkling

Preheat the oven to 400°F. Line 2 baking sheets with parchment and set aside.

Combine the white spelt flour, ground millet flour, salt, and baking soda in the bowl of a food processor fitted with the dough blade and pulse to combine. Add the coconut oil and pulse to incorporate. With the food processor running, drizzle in the water a little at a time, just until the mixture begins to pull together. You may not use all of the water.

Turn the dough out onto a lightly floured surface and gather it into a ball. Knead gently once or twice. If the dough is a little sticky, knead in a bit more flour but try not to overwork the dough. Roll out the dough until it is slightly less than ⅛ inch thick.

Prick the dough all over with a fork. Cut into 2-inch squares and carefully place them on the prepared baking sheets, leaving ½ inch between crackers. Mist the tops of the crackers with water, then sprinkle them with the flaked salt.

Bake until the crackers are slightly brown on the edges, 10 to 15 minutes, rotating the baking sheets halfway through baking. Let the crackers cool on a wire rack.

For *gluten-free* Salty Water Crackers, replace the white spelt flour with an equal amount of gluten-free all-purpose baking mix.

These crackers are naturally *vegan*.

wheat crackers

ABOUT 70 CRACKERS

These thin crackers are great with cheese or dips, or to just nibble on their own. A tiny bit of vanilla helps create the subtly malty flavor Wheat Thins are known for. I like to replace a fourth cup of the whole-wheat flour with an equal amount of barley flour for an even nuttier taste. For an added twist, sprinkle on a little of the Ranch Flavoring (page 151).

1¼ cups (150 grams) whole-wheat flour

2 teaspoons cane sugar

½ teaspoon salt

Pinch of turmeric

2 tablespoons olive oil

1 teaspoon brown rice syrup or golden syrup

¼ cup (2 ounces) water

¼ teaspoon vanilla

Olive oil spray

Flake salt and freshly ground pepper

Preheat the oven to 400°F. Line 2 baking sheets with parchment and set aside.

Combine the whole-wheat flour, sugar, salt, and turmeric in the bowl of a food processor fitted with the dough blade. Pulse several times to mix thoroughly. Drizzle in the olive oil and pulse to combine. With the food processor running, add the brown rice syrup, water, and vanilla. Mix until smooth.

Turn the dough out onto a well-floured surface. Divide it into 2 pieces. Keep the dough you aren't working with covered with plastic wrap. Working with one dough ball at a time, roll out the dough until it is about ⅛ inch thick. Place the dough onto prepared baking sheets. Using a pastry wheel or knife, cut the dough into 1-by-1-inch crackers, but don't separate them. Prick each cracker with a fork. Repeat with the remaining dough.

Spray the crackers with olive oil spray and sprinkle them with salt and pepper.

Bake until the edges of the crackers are golden brown, about 10 minutes. Cool the sheets of crackers completely on a wire rack before breaking them into individual crackers.

For gluten-free Wheat Crackers (though not really wheat), replace the whole-wheat flour with an equal amount of gluten-free all-purpose baking mix. Roll out the dough between two pieces of parchment for easier rolling.

These crackers are naturally vegan.

cheesy squares

ABOUT 70 CRACKERS

These crackers are packed with cheese flavor, even if they aren't bright orange. For a traditional cheddar flavor, use a good sharp cheddar (I like Beecher's Flagship). Or go a little crazy and use a stronger cheese like Camembert. For an even cheesier flavor, sprinkle with Cheese Powder (page 153).

4 ounces grated sharp cheddar cheese

2 tablespoons (¼ stick) unsalted butter

½ cup (60 grams) whole-grain spelt flour or white whole-wheat flour

¼ cup (30 grams) all-purpose or white spelt flour

⅛ teaspoon Onion Powder (page 149)

¼ teaspoon salt

2 tablespoons milk, plus more for brushing

Preheat the oven to 350°F. Line 2 baking sheets with parchment and set aside.

Combine the cheese, butter, whole-grain spelt flour, all-purpose flour, onion powder, salt, and milk in the bowl of a food processor fitted with the dough blade. Pulse to form a ball, 1 to 2 minutes. If the dough appears oily from the cheese, wrap it in plastic wrap and chill for 30 minutes.

Turn the dough out onto a well-floured surface. Roll out the dough until it is ⅛ to ¹⁄₁₆ inch thick. Brush the dough with the milk. Using a pastry wheel or knife, cut the dough into 1-by-1-inch squares. Prick the center of each cracker with a skewer. Place the crackers on the prepared baking sheets, leaving at least ½ inch between crackers.

Bake until the crackers are just slightly brown on the edges, about 10 minutes, rotating the baking sheets halfway through baking. The crackers will crisp up as they cool, so be careful not to overbake them. Cool the crackers completely on a wire rack.

For *gluten-free* Cheesy Squares, replace the whole-grain spelt and all-purpose flours with an equal amount of gluten-free all-purpose baking mix. Roll out the dough between two pieces of parchment for easier rolling.

These Cheesy Squares are packed with cheese and don't translate well without it. For a *vegan* alternative, follow the vegan instructions for Cheesy Fish (page 85), but cut into little squares.

savory crackers

ABOUT 50 CRACKERS

My high school boyfriend was obsessed with Chicken in a Biskit crackers. It's not surprising since they are packed with flavor and MSG. These crackers skip the MSG but still have tons of flavor from the herbs and spices.

½ cup (60 grams) all-purpose flour

¼ cup (30 grams) rye or whole-wheat flour

¼ cup (30 grams) chickpea or whole-wheat flour

Pinch of baking powder

3 teaspoons cane sugar, divided

2 teaspoons salt, divided

2 tablespoons plus 2 teaspoons nutritional yeast, divided

4 tablespoons (½ stick) unsalted butter, at room temperature and cut into pieces

¼ cup (2 ounces) warm milk (about 120°F)

1 teaspoon finely chopped chives

½ tablespoon Onion Powder (page 149)

½ teaspoon Garlic Powder (page 149)

¼ teaspoon dried thyme

½ teaspoon dried sage

Pinch of paprika

Preheat the oven to 400°F. Line 2 baking sheets with parchment and set aside.

Sift the all-purpose flour, rye flour, chickpea flour, baking powder, 2 teaspoons of the sugar, 1 teaspoon of the salt, and 2 teaspoons of the nutritional yeast together and set aside.

Put the butter in the bowl of a stand mixer fitted with the paddle attachment. Pour the warm milk over the butter. Add half of the flour mixture and mix on medium speed until combined, about 1 minute. With the mixer running, stir in the chives and the remaining flour mixture, ¼ cup at a time, until the dough forms into a ball and pulls away from the sides of the bowl, about 2 minutes.

Combine the onion powder, garlic powder, thyme, sage, paprika, and the remaining 1 teaspoon of sugar, 1 teaspoon of salt, and 2 tablespoons of nutritional yeast in a spice grinder or blender. Blend to create a fine powder and set aside.

On a lightly floured surface, roll out the dough until it is ⅛ inch thick. Sprinkle with half of the spice mixture and lightly roll to press the spices into the dough. Prick the dough all over with a fork. Cut the dough into 1-by-2-inch rectangles with a pastry wheel or sharp knife and carefully place the crackers on the prepared baking sheets.

Bake until the crackers are a very light golden brown, 10 to 12 minutes, rotating the baking sheets halfway through baking. While the crackers are still warm, place them in a paper bag and sprinkle with the remaining spice mixture. Shake lightly to coat and spread the crackers onto a baking sheet to cool before serving.

For gluten-free Savory Crackers, replace the all-purpose and rye flowers with an equal amount of gluten-free all-purpose baking mix. Roll out the dough between two pieces of parchment for easier rolling.

For vegan Savory Crackers, replace the butter with an equal amount of coconut oil and the milk with an equal amount of water or soy milk.

CHIPS

potato chips

ABOUT 10 CUPS CHIPS

Russet potatoes are the quintessential frying potato, but I recommend trying this recipe with a mix of other starchy vegetables like lotus root, parsnips, or yams. Pull out your mandolin for the thinnest, crispiest chips. Or look for special ridged chip cutters to make your own ruffled version. For traditional chips, fry the potato rounds; for less greasy (but still tasty) chips, bake them instead.

3 medium russet potatoes (about 1½ pounds)

Safflower oil, for frying

About 3 tablespoons salt, Sour Cream and Onion Flavoring (page 150), or BBQ Flavoring (page 150)

Slice the potatoes into ¹⁄₁₆-inch-thick rounds and place in a large bowl. Cover the potato slices with cold water, swish, and drain. Place the slices in a single layer on a towel and top with another towel. Gently press to dry the slices. Repeat with the remaining slices.

To fry the chips, heat at least 2 inches of oil in a heavy-bottomed pot to 375°F. Fry the dried potato slices in batches, being sure not to crowd the pot, for 1 to 2 minutes, flipping once, until they are a light golden brown and the bubbling oil calms. If there is still bubbling going on, there is still moisture in the chips and they will be soggy. Remove the chips with a slotted spoon and place on a wire rack to drain and cool slightly. Sprinkle to taste with your chosen seasoning and serve.

To bake the chips, preheat the oven to 400°F. Spray the dried potato slices with olive oil. Bake until the chips are a light golden brown, about 10 minutes, rotating the baking sheet halfway through baking. Sprinkle to taste with your chosen seasoning and serve.

These chips are naturally *gluten-free* and *vegan.*

corn chip strips

ABOUT 4 CUPS CHIPS

Fritos are one of the few packaged products out there made from real food: they're just corn, corn oil, and salt. These corn chips are almost as simple, but have a slightly more complex flavor. Look for masa harina in the Mexican food aisle of most well-stocked grocery stores. To refreshen day-old chips, simply toast them for five minutes in a 350°F oven.

1 cup (150 grams) masa harina

2 tablespoons flaxseed oil

½ cup (4 ounces) water

½ teaspoon salt

Pinch of cayenne pepper (optional)

Safflower oil, for frying

Salt

Combine the masa harina, flaxseed oil, water, salt, and cayenne pepper, if using, in the bowl of a food processor fitted with the dough blade. Pulse until a crumbly dough forms, about 1 minute.

Turn the dough out onto a wooden cutting board dusted with masa harina and gather it into a ball. Divide the dough ball into 4 pieces. Keep the dough you aren't working with covered with plastic wrap. Working with one dough ball at a time, place the dough on the prepared cutting board. Roll out the dough until it is slightly less than ¼ inch thick. Prick the dough all over with a fork and cut it into ¾-by-1½-inch rectangles.

Heat at least 1½ inches of oil in a heavy-bottomed pot to 350°F. Using a spatula or bench scraper, carefully transfer the dough rectangles to the oil. Fry the chips until they are a light golden brown, about 1 minute, turning once or twice. Remove the chips with a slotted spoon and place on a wire rack to drain. Repeat with the remaining dough.

Once the chips are slightly cooled, transfer them to a small paper bag. Season to taste with salt and shake to coat.

These chips are naturally *gluten-free* and *vegan*.

nacho cheese tortilla chips

ABOUT 70 CHIPS

As tempting as they may be, skip the bag of Doritos and pick up a package or two of corn tortillas, pull out the fryer, and feast on your own cheesy, spicy chips free from FD&C Red #40, corn syrup solids, and both kinds of glutamate. For Ranch Tortilla Chips, simply replace the spice mix with Ranch Flavoring (page 151). These chips will be just as delicious the next day if you toast them for five minutes in a 350°F oven before serving.

1 teaspoon Onion Powder (page 149)

1 teaspoon Garlic Powder (page 149)

¼ teaspoon dried mustard

½ teaspoon turbinado or cane sugar

1 teaspoon chili powder

½ teaspoon cayenne pepper

½ teaspoon paprika

1 teaspoon nutritional yeast

½ teaspoon dried oregano

½ teaspoon dried sage

8 teaspoons Cheese Powder (page 153)

1 teaspoon salt

½ teaspoon black pepper

Safflower oil, for frying

12 corn tortillas

Place the onion powder, garlic powder, dried mustard, sugar, chili powder, cayenne pepper, paprika, nutritional yeast, oregano, sage, Cheese Powder, salt, and black pepper into a spice grinder or food processor and pulse until well blended. Set aside.

Preheat the oven to 350°F. Line a baking sheet with parchment and set aside.

Heat at least 1½ inches of oil in a heavy-bottomed pot to 350°F. While the oil is heating, slice the tortillas into triangles or rectangle strips. Fry the tortilla pieces in batches, being sure not to crowd the pot, until the bubbling slows, about 1 minute. Remove the chips with a slotted spoon and place them in a paper bag. Sprinkle with the reserved spice mix and shake to coat. Pour the coated chips onto the prepared baking sheet and bake for 5 minutes to crisp.

These chips are naturally gluten-free.

For vegan Nacho Cheese Tortilla Chips, omit the Cheese Powder. You'll have a less cheesy, but equally delicious, snack.

crunchy cheese puffs

3 TO 4 CUPS PUFFS

It's no small feat to create perfectly textured Crunchy Cheese Puffs. First you make one of the weirdest doughs you've ever made. Then you steam it. Then you dry it. And then, only then, do you fry it. But I think somewhere out there are people like me who are just nutty enough to take on the challenge. Do be aware that the puffs need to dry for up to 10 hours so plan accordingly.

½ cup (90 grams) tapioca starch

⅛ cup (20 grams) finely ground corn flour (not masa harina)

1 teaspoon salt

1 teaspoon cane sugar

1 ounce grated, loosely packed sharp cheddar cheese (or cheese of your choice), melted with 1 table-spoon of water

⅛ to ¼ cup (1 to 2 ounces) hot water, plus more for steaming

Safflower oil, for frying

Salt

Cheese Powder (page 153)

Bring a large pot of water, fitted with a steamer tray, to a boil. Line the steamer with a lightly oiled sheet of parchment.

Combine the tapioca starch, corn flour, salt, and sugar in the bowl of a food processor fitted with the dough blade. Add the melted cheese and pulse until the mixture resembles breadcrumbs. With the food processor running, drizzle in the hot water until a thick dough starts to form and pull away a little from the sides of the bowl. The texture will be quite strange—a little like cheese or tofu in consistency—and it will ooze if left sitting.

Pull the dough together and place it in the center of the parchment in the steamer. Lightly press it down to about ¼ inch thick. Steam until the dough is rubbery and slightly translucent throughout, 45 minutes to 1 hour.

Remove the parchment with the dough still on it and let it cool to room tempera-ture. Remove the dough from the parchment, flip it over, and let it stand to dry slightly. Once the dough is not too sticky to handle, slice it into ¼-by-¾-inch strips, rolling each strip between your fingers a little to round it.

Place the dough pieces on the tray of a food dehydrator and dehydrate until the sticks are crisp throughout, 6 to 10 hours. (If you don't have a dehydrator, place the sticks on a parchment-lined baking sheet and bake at 150°F—or as low as your oven will go—with the door slightly propped open, for 6 to 8 hours. Once the sticks are completely dried, you can store them in an airtight container for up to 3 months.

When you are ready to fry your puffs, place a wire rack over a baking sheet. Heat at least 2½ inches of oil in a heavy-bottomed pot to 370°F. Fry the sticks in batches of 6 to 10 (depending on the size of your pot), until they puff and the bubbling oil calms, about 30 seconds to a minute. Remove the puffs with a slotted spoon and place them on the rack to cool. Test a puff. If it's a little chewy, fry the next batch a bit longer. Repeat with the remaining sticks. Place the puffs in a paper bag, season generously to taste with salt and Cheese Powder, and shake the bag gently to coat.

These puffs are naturally gluten-free.

Although not really cheesy, you can make vegan Onion Puffs by adding 1 tablespoon Onion Powder (page 149) plus a teaspoon of dried green onions to the flours and leaving out the cheese. You'll need to increase the hot water to ⅓ cup. Sprinkle the fried puffs with nutritional yeast and salt to taste instead of the Cheese Powder.

cheesy popcorn

3 TO 4 CUPS POPCORN

Every so often, I indulge in one of my favorite solo dinners: Curled up on the couch, eating an enormous bowl of popcorn. I prefer popcorn made in a pot on the stove, and shaken with enough Cheese Powder to coat my fingers with each bite.

1 tablespoon coconut or safflower oil

⅓ cup unpopped popcorn

Olive oil spray

¼ cup Cheese Powder (page 153)

1 teaspoon sea salt

Place the oil in a heavy-bottomed pot over medium heat just until it melts. Add the popcorn, cover, and shake every now and then until the popping stops. Place the popcorn in a bowl and spray it with a bit of olive oil spray. Sprinkle with the Cheese Powder and salt.

This popcorn is naturally *gluten-free*.

For a tasty *vegan* Cheesy Popcorn, replace the Cheese Powder with 2 tablespoons nutritional yeast or to taste.

crunchy pretzel sticks

24 TO 30 CUPS PRETZELS

Pretzel sticks take on a whole new life when you make them with something other than standard white flour. I love this mix of whole-wheat, bread, and barley flours. For a different flavor, skip the egg wash and lightly brush each pretzel stick with a mixture made from 1 tablespoon honey and ½ teaspoon dry mustard before baking.

¼ cup (30 grams) whole-wheat or rye flour

1 cup (120 grams) bread flour

¼ cup (30 grams) barley flour

½ cup (4 ounces) plus 1 tablespoon water, divided

¼ teaspoon active dry yeast

½ teaspoon rapadura or cane sugar

1 tablespoon brown rice syrup

¼ teaspoon salt

1 egg white

½ tablespoon baking soda

2 tablespoons coarse sea salt

Sift the whole-wheat flour, bread flour, and barley flour together and set aside.

Warm ½ cup of the water to 115°F. In the bowl of a stand mixer fitted with the paddle attachment, combine the warm water, yeast, sugar, and brown rice syrup. Mix well on low speed and let stand for 5 minutes. Add the salt and half of the flour mixture and mix on low speed to create a loose dough, about 1 to 2 minutes. Switch to the dough hook and, with the mixer on low speed, add the remaining flour mixture a little at a time until the dough comes together into a ball. Increase the mixer speed to high and knead for 3 minutes. Punch down the dough and continue to knead on medium-low speed for another 2 minutes, until the dough is smooth and not sticky. If the dough is very sticky, add a bit more bread flour.

Cover the dough and let it proof for 1 hour in a warm spot.

Preheat the oven to 375°F. Line 2 baking sheets with parchment and set aside.

Divide the dough into 4 pieces. Keep the dough you aren't working with covered. Working with one piece at a time, pinch off tablespoon-sized pieces of dough and roll into long ¼-inch-thick logs. Place the logs on the prepared baking sheets. Repeat with the remaining dough.

In a small bowl, whisk the egg whites with the baking soda and remaining 1 tablespoon water. Brush each pretzel generously with the egg wash and sprinkle with the coarse salt.

Bake until the pretzels are a deep golden brown, 10 to 15 minutes, rotating the baking sheets every 5 minutes. Cool on a wire rack, and serve long or break into smaller sticks.

. . . .

to make peanut butter–stuffed pretzels, prepare the pretzel

dough as directed, but roll the dough into a ⅛-inch-thick rectangle. Cut the rolled dough into 1½-by-1½-inch squares. Place ¼ teaspoon of peanut butter in the center of each piece of pretzel dough and roll the dough around the peanut butter filling, pinching the edges together to seal. Place the filled pretzels, seam side down, on a parchment-lined baking sheet. Brush with the egg mixture, sprinkle with coarse salt, and bake in a 425°F oven until the pretzels are a deep golden brown, about 15 minutes, rotating the baking sheet every 5 minutes. Cool on a wire rack.

For gluten-free Crunchy Pretzel Sticks, replace the whole-wheat, bread, and barley flours with an equal weight of gluten-free all-purpose baking mix plus 1 tablespoon freshly ground chia seeds mixed with 2 tablespoons water. The dough won't have the same elasticity as the wheat-based dough, so you'll need to work with the dough very carefully. For gluten-free Peanut Butter–Stuffed Pretzels, roll the dough between two pieces of parchment paper dusted with gluten-free flour.

For vegan Crunchy Pretzel Sticks, skip the egg white and mix the baking soda with an additional tablespoon of water before brushing it on the pretzels.

DIPS

onion dip

1 CUP DIP

Forget those little packets of spice mixes stirred into sour cream. While this dip may take a bit more time, it's hardly what you could call hard work, and slowly caramelized onions put those little dehydrated ones to complete shame.

1 tablespoon unsalted butter

1 cup chopped onion

½ cup sour cream

Salt and freshly ground pepper

Pinch of smoked paprika (optional)

Splash of buttermilk (optional)

Place the butter in a heavy skillet and melt over medium-low heat. Add the onion and a pinch of salt and, stirring occasionally, let the onions sweat and caramelize, 20 to 30 minutes. Don't be tempted to turn up the heat; you want it low and slow to get the onions to their sweetest without charring.

Once the onions are an even golden color, remove them from the heat and allow them to cool to room temperature. You can put them in the refrigerator, covered, to speed up the process.

Once the onions are cool, stir them and any collected juices into the sour cream and season to taste with salt and pepper, and a pinch of smoked paprika if using. If the consistency is too thick, add a splash of buttermilk to thin it out. You can eat this dip immediately, but I think it's even better after sitting, covered in the refrigerator, for an hour or two to let the flavors meld.

This dip is naturally *gluten-free*.

For *vegan* Onion Dip, replace the butter with an equal amount of olive oil and the sour cream with an equal amount of Vegan Cashew Cream (page 154) or smoothly pureed silken tofu.

pimento cheese

Pimentos are sweet peppers with a flavor subtly different than a typical bell pepper. They are slightly sweeter, without the bitter edge that bells can sometimes have. Pimentos are delicious when paired with a good sharp cheddar cheese. If you can't find fresh pimentos, you can substitute just about any fresh sweet pepper. For a creamier spread, mix in two tablespoons of cream cheese.

2 pimento peppers, finely diced

4 ounces grated sharp cheddar cheese

Salt

In a medium bowl by hand, or in the bowl of a food processor, mix the peppers and cheese. Season to taste with the salt. Allow the mixture to sit in the refrigerator, covered, for 1 hour to allow the flavors to meld.

This cheese is naturally gluten-free.

For vegan Pimento Spread, simmer 2 cups grated carrot with 2 cups hemp milk (or other non-dairy milk) and ¼ teaspoon salt until the carrots soften and start to melt into the liquid, about 10 minutes. Remove the mixture from the heat and cool to room temperature. Once cool, mix in 1 cup Vegan Cashew Cream (page 154), 2 finely diced pimento peppers, and salt and pepper to taste.

chile con queso

It's hard for me to imagine a more perfect food than chile con queso. The melty, creamy cheese with plenty of kick from chiles is heavenly whether spread on a chip or poured over a piece of toast. To make sure your dip is creamy and not grainy, it is important not to rush the melting.

1 tablespoon unsalted butter

½ cup chopped onion

½ cup canned green chiles

1 medium tomato, peeled, seeded, and chopped

½ teaspoon dried oregano

¼ cup (2 ounces) heavy cream

½ cup (4 ounces) buttermilk

1 teaspoon white spelt flour

2 ounces grated Monterey Jack, Colby, or cheddar cheese

⅛ cup (1 ounce) crumbled queso fresco or Cotija

Salt and freshly ground pepper

Combine the butter, onion, and chiles in a sauté pan over medium heat and cook until the onion softens and becomes translucent, about 5 minutes. Stir in the tomato and oregano and cook for 1 minute.

Stir in the cream, buttermilk, and flour and bring to a simmer to thicken slightly, about 3 minutes. Stir in the Monterey Jack cheese and gently stir to melt. Season to taste with salt and pepper. Serve immediately, topped with the queso fresco.

For gluten-free Chile Con Queso, replace the spelt flour with an equal amount of arrowroot powder.

For a vegan alternative to Chile Con Queso, make the vegan version of the Onion Dip (page 116), and stir in a tablespoon of pickled chile peppers (like Mama Lil's).

bean dip

1½ CUPS DIP

Forget about those cans of brown mush that look more like dog than people food. This dip is flavorful and beautiful, in a dip sort of way. Instead of using the traditional pinto beans, I prefer to use red lentils, which retain a little of their rosy color. Black-eyed peas are also great in this recipe, but if you aren't starting with canned peas, make sure you soak the peas overnight and then drain them before proceeding with the recipe.

1 cup dried lentils

¼ onion

2 tablespoons olive oil, plus more for drizzling

1½ tablespoons freshly squeezed lemon juice

¼ cup chopped chives or scallions

Salt and freshly ground pepper

Combine the lentils and onion in a heavy-bottomed saucepan. Add enough water to cover the lentils. Bring to a boil and then reduce to a simmer. Cover the saucepan and cook on low until the lentils are quite soft and have lost any of their mealy texture, 5 to 10 minutes, adding a little more water if the lentils look dry. Remove from the heat and let the lentils cool.

Remove the onion and discard. Add the olive oil and lemon juice and mash the mixture with a fork. Transfer the dip to a bowl and stir in the chives. Season to taste with salt and pepper, and drizzle with olive oil before serving.

This dip is naturally *gluten-free* and *vegan*.

OTHER

corn nuts

ABOUT 2 CUPS CORN NUTS

My version of this classic bar staple skips both the soaking of the dried hominy kernels and the frying. It depends on high-quality canned hominy, which is easily found in the Mexican food aisle of most grocery stores. I like to use Spanish paprika for a bit of smokiness, but if you prefer the more traditional flavor, simply season with sea salt. Note that these corn nuts aren't the teeth-crackingly hard kind you may be used to. If frying is your thing, you can fry the drained, dried, and unseasoned kernels in 375°F vegetable oil and season as directed.

1 can (24 ounces) hominy
½ teaspoon Spanish paprika
½ teaspoon sea salt
Dash of Onion Powder (page 149)
Dash of Garlic Powder (page 149)
2 tablespoons olive oil

Rinse the hominy until the water runs clear. Spread the drained kernels onto a baking sheet to dry for about 30 minutes. (Dry kernels will bake up more crisply than wet ones.)

While the hominy is drying, preheat the oven to 400°F. Line a baking sheet with foil and set aside.

In a medium bowl, combine the paprika, salt, onion powder, and garlic powder. Add the hominy and stir to coat evenly.

Pour the hominy onto the prepared baking sheet and spread it evenly. Drizzle with the olive oil. To help keep too many kernels from escaping as they heat and pop, place another baking sheet across the top at a slight angle to allow steam to escape. Bake until the kernels are crisp, 20 to 30 minutes, stirring every once in a while so that they roast evenly.

These corn nuts are naturally *gluten-free* and *vegan*.

crescent rolls

16 ROLLS

A basket of hot, fluffy crescent rolls makes a perfect addition to any meal. These rolls freeze well, so make a double batch for a hot snack anytime. I also like to use this dough to create pimento cheese rolls: Simply roll the dough out into a large rectangle, cover it with Pimento Cheese (page 117), roll it up and slice it cinnamon roll–style, and bake as directed.

¼ cup (2 ounces) milk

2 tablespoons cane sugar

½ teaspoon salt

3 tablespoons unsalted butter

2½ to 3 cups (300 to 350 grams) white spelt or all-purpose flour

½ cup (80 grams) oat or cake flour

1 teaspoon baking powder

½ cup (4 ounces) warm water

2 teaspoons active dry yeast

1 egg

Melted butter, for brushing

In a heavy-bottomed pot, heat the milk just until it starts to boil, then remove it from the heat. Stir in the sugar, salt, and butter, and set aside to cool.

Sift the white spelt flour, oat flour, and baking powder together and set aside.

Place the warm water into the bowl of a stand mixer fitted with the paddle attachment and sprinkle with the yeast. Let stand for 3 minutes. Stir in half of the flour mixture by hand. Mix in the cooled milk mixture and the egg. Continue to add the flour, ¼ cup at a time, until you have a soft, moist dough that just pulls away from the sides of the mixing bowl. You may need a little more or less flour.

Switch to the dough hook and knead on high speed for 2 minutes, adding a little flour as needed to keep the dough from sticking to the sides of the bowl.

Place the dough into a buttered bowl, turn it once to coat, and cover with plastic wrap. Refrigerate for at least 2 hours, or up to 2 days.

Line 2 baking sheets with parchment and set aside. Turn the dough out onto a lightly floured surface. Divide the dough in half. Keep the dough you aren't working with covered with plastic wrap. Working with one piece at a time, roll the dough out to a large circle about ¼ inch thick. Slice the dough as you would a pie, into 8 wedges. Roll each piece from the wide side to the point, pinch to close, and place on the prepared baking sheets, leaving 2 inches between each roll. Repeat with the remaining dough. If the points begin to loosen, brush a little water under them to help them reseal.

Cover and let rise for 1 hour in a warm, draft-free spot. Preheat the oven to 400°F.

Brush the tops of each roll with melted butter. Bake until the rolls are golden brown, about 15 minutes. Cool on a wire rack for a minute or two, and serve warm.

For gluten-free Crescent Rolls, replace the white spelt flour with an equal amount of gluten-free all-purpose baking mix, stir 2 tablespoons freshly ground chia seeds into the milk mixture, and add an additional egg and an additional tablespoon of butter. Skip the dough hook, and mix the dough only with the paddle attachment, for about 4 minutes. Add a bit more flour if the dough doesn't start to pull away from the sides of the bowl. The dough will be very moist, but don't be tempted to add more flour than is required. Pull the dough into a ball, and let rise at room temperature for 1 hour. Then, roll between two pieces of parchment and follow the main instructions to roll and bake.

For vegan Crescent Rolls, replace the milk with an equal amount of almond or soy milk and the butter with an equal amount of coconut oil. You can leave out the egg, or for a richer dough, replace it with 1 teaspoon ground chia or flaxseed whisked with 3 tablespoons water.

hot pockets

8 POCKETS

One of my favorite dinners when I was growing up was pasties—little pastry hand pies filled with stew, pizza toppings, or ham and cheese. We always customized the ingredients in our pasties and marked each pie with a letter so that we'd know whose was whose. The invention of Hot Pockets took most of the work out of making these savory little hand pies, but they are nowhere near as tasty as the homemade version. This recipe makes a simple ham and cheese pie, but the tender dough makes a great crust for just about any filling.

1 batch Crescent Roll dough (page 123)

8 thin slices provolone or Monterey Jack cheese, cut in half

8 thin slices ham

Melted butter, for brushing

Prepare the Crescent Roll dough as directed, but instead of rolling the dough into 2 circles, roll it into two 9-by-6-inch rectangles about ¼ inch thick. Cut each rectangle into thirds, creating 3-by-6-inch rectangles. Place a piece of cheese and a piece of ham, folding as needed, on each of the dough pieces. Fold them over to create 3-by-3-inch squares. Press the edges with the tines of a fork to seal and place on parchment-lined baking sheets, leaving 2 inches between each square.

Cover and let rise for 1 hour in a warm, draft-free spot. Preheat the oven to 400°F.

Brush the tops of each pocket with melted butter and bake until the pockets are golden brown, about 15 minutes. Cooled pockets can be frozen and reheated in a 375°F oven for 15 minutes for a great anytime snack.

Use the *gluten-free* or *vegan* version of the Crescent Roll dough (page 124) to create gluten-free or vegan Hot Pockets, and fill with ingredients you love!

potato sticks

ABOUT 4 CUPS STICKS

These homemade Potato Sticks taste more like French fries than those straight out of the can, but with an addictive crunch. I like to amp up the flavor (and nutrition) by adding a sweet potato to the mix.

2 medium russet potatoes (1 pound), julienned

1 medium sweet potato or yam (½ pound), julienned (optional)

1 teaspoon sea salt

1 tablespoon potato flour

Safflower or peanut oil, for frying

¼ teaspoon Onion Powder (page 149)

Salt and freshly ground pepper

Place the julienned russet potatoes and sweet potato, if using, in a bowl of cold water and let them soak for 1 minute. Drain well through a fine sieve. Transfer the potatoes to a bowl and sprinkle with the salt. Pour the potatoes in an even layer onto a linen towel and cover with another towel. Gently press to remove the water. Transfer the potatoes back to the bowl, add the potato flour, and stir to coat.

Heat at least 2 inches of oil in a heavy-bottomed pot to 370°F. Preheat the oven to 400°F. Line a baking sheet with parchment and set aside.

Fry the sticks in 1-cup batches until golden brown, about 1 to 2 minutes. Remove the sticks with a slotted spoon and place them on the prepared baking sheet. Season with a pinch of the onion powder and salt and pepper to taste. Repeat with the remaining sticks. Bake until crunchy and deep golden in color, about 5 minutes.

Let the potato sticks cool on the baking sheet and serve immediately. Leftover sticks can be stored in an airtight container for up to 1 week. If they lose their crunch, reheat in a 400°F oven for 5 to 6 minutes.

> These potato sticks are naturally *gluten-free* and *vegan*.

potato tots

ABOUT 100 TOTS

Traditional tots are made from russet potatoes, but I like to grate in a little bit of sweet potato or yam. Keeping the skins on helps to preserve some of the nutrients, so give your potatoes a good scrub instead of a peel. This recipe, adapted from one by Cooks Country *magazine, churns out light, fluffy tots with a crispy crust every time. The corn flour and ground millet flour give the tots a little extra crunch, but it's OK to substitute whole-wheat flour if you prefer.*

5 to 6 medium russet potatoes (2 pound), cut into chunks

1 medium sweet potato or yam (¼ pound), cut into chunks

2 cups cold water

2½ teaspoons kosher salt, divided

2 teaspoons corn flour

2 teaspoons ground millet flour

Pinch of cayenne pepper

Salt and freshly ground black pepper

Safflower or peanut oil, for frying

Place the russet potatoes and sweet potato into the bowl of a food processor fitted with a metal cutting blade. Pulse 5 or 6 times until coarsely ground.

In a large bowl, combine the cold water and 2 teaspoons of the salt. Add the potatoes and stir to coat. Drain well through a fine sieve, pushing out as much water as you can.

Transfer the potatoes to a microwave-safe bowl and heat for 4 minutes. Stir and heat for another 4 minutes. Stir in the corn flour, ground millet flour, cayenne, and the remaining ½ teaspoon salt.

Line a 9-inch square pan with parchment and pour in the potato mixture. Spread it evenly and let the mixture cool to room temperature. Chill in the freezer for 20 minutes.

Once the potato mixture is frozen, cut it into 1-by-½-inch tots. Line a baking sheet with parchment and set aside.

Heat at least 2 inches of oil in a heavy-bottomed pot to 370°F. Fry the tots in batches, being sure not to crowd the pot, until golden brown, about 1 to 2 minutes. Remove the tots with a slotted spoon and place them on the prepared baking

sheet. While they are still hot, season them to taste with salt and pepper. Repeat with the remaining tots.

Serve immediately or, to freeze for storage, let the tots cool on the baking sheet. Once the baking sheet is cool, place it in the freezer for 1 hour. Transfer the frozen tots to a resealable storage bag and keep them in the freezer for up to 3 months. Before serving, reheat in a 400°F oven until crispy, about 5 to 8 minutes.

These tots are naturally *gluten-free* and *vegan*.

the real snacks
PANTRY

All Pantry
recipes are
naturally gluten-
free and vegan
unless a variation
is offered

Caramel Sauce

Chocolate Syrup

CHEE

powdered sugar

Although homemade powdered sugar will never be quite the same as the blindingly white stuff you buy at the store, I think the difference in flavor will convert you. Plus, it's easier to make than you might think. Any fine-grain sugar will work; try using a fine beet sugar or granulated fructose if you want bright white powdered sugar, or opt for rapadura (which has a great, rich flavor) if color is not as important to you.

ABOUT ¾ CUP SUGAR

1 cup (about 200 grams) sugar

½ teaspoon cornstarch or arrowroot powder

Place the sugar in a blender, up to 1 cup at a time, adding the cornstarch to help keep the sugar from caking, and pulse until you get the desired texture. Stop the blender occasionally and shake it, to make sure no sugar crystals are stuck in the corners, before continuing to blend. To get the finest powder, blend for 5 to 10 minutes. Let the sugar settle for a minute or two before removing the lid, or you may end up inhaling sugar dust. Keeps well in an airtight container for months.

sugar syrup

Before I tell you how to replace it, let me start with a word or two on corn syrup. Typically, corn syrup that you buy in the store is not the same as the high-fructose corn syrup that is so prevalent in processed foods. Corn syrup is simply fructose made from corn that has been converted to keep in a non-crystallized form. Inverted sugars, like corn syrup, are important in creating smooth textures in candies and confections. However, corn syrup doesn't add much nutritional value, and it is a high glycemic index sugar. Instead, you can make your own sugar syrup from evaporated cane sugar, a little acid (such as lemon juice), and water. I like to also add a little brown rice syrup in mine to help prevent crystallization, but you can make this syrup without it as well.

ABOUT 1 PINT SYRUP

2 cups (400 grams) cane sugar

½ teaspoon cream of tartar or freshly squeezed lemon juice

1 teaspoon brown rice syrup (optional)

½ cup water

Combine the sugar, cream of tartar, brown rice syrup, if using, and water in a heavy-bottomed pot, stir to combine, and affix a candy thermometer to the side of the pot

Over medium heat, bring the mixture to a boil. Use a moistened pastry brush to brush down any errant crystals that form on the side of the pot. Do not stir.

Continue to simmer, making sure no crystals form, until the mixture reaches 238°F. Remove from heat, moving the mixture as little as possible, and let cool without touching. This syrup can be stored in an airtight container at room temperature indefinitely, but it will crystallize over time.

sweetened condensed milk

While it may be simpler to just pick up a can, homemade sweetened condensed milk is far more satisfying (and you know where your milk is coming from!). Even better, you can cook it an hour or so longer and make your own irresistible Dulce de Leche.

ABOUT 1 CUP MILK

1½ cups (12 ounces) whole milk

½ cup (100 grams) turbinado sugar

½ tablespoon unsalted butter

½ teaspoon vanilla

Place the milk and sugar in a heavy-bottomed pot over medium-low heat. Stirring often to prevent scorching, bring to a low simmer. When you begin to see steam, reduce the temperature to low and continue to cook until the mixture has reduced to a little less than 1 cup and is a light tan color, about 2 hours, checking in and stirring every so often.

Remove the pan from the heat and stir in the butter and vanilla. Cool before storing, covered, in the refrigerator, for up to 2 weeks.

Coconut milk makes the creamiest vegan variation of Sweetened Condensed Milk. Use a whole can of regular, not "lite" coconut milk, and mix the heavier coconut cream into the lighter coconut milk before reducing. Leave out the butter. Other non-dairy milks yield a caramely syrup that tastes great but lacks the creaminess coconut milk gives.

evaporated milk

Evaporated milk is sweetened condensed milk's unsweetened cousin. Milk is ever so slowly heated to reduce to a slightly thicker version of itself.

ABOUT 1 CUP MILK

1½ cups milk

Place the milk in a heavy-bottomed pot over medium-low heat. Stirring often to prevent scorching, bring to a low simmer. When you begin to see steam, reduce the temperature to low and continue to cook until the mixture has reduced to a little less than 1 cup, about 2 hours, checking in and stirring every so often. Cool before storing, covered, in the refrigerator, for up to 2 weeks.

> For *vegan* Evaporated Milk, replace the milk with an equal amount of coconut milk (not "lite" coconut milk).

. . . .

chocolate syrup

For the perfect mocha or glass of chocolate milk, try this homemade chocolate syrup.

ABOUT 1 CUP SYRUP

½ cup water

2 tablespoons muscavado or cane sugar

¼ cup brown rice syrup or Sugar Syrup (page 135)

¼ cup cocoa powder

1 teaspoon espresso powder (optional)

Pinch of salt

2 ounces bittersweet or semisweet chocolate, finely chopped

In a heavy-bottomed pot over medium heat, combine the water, sugar, and brown rice syrup. Whisk in the cocoa powder, espresso powder, if using, and salt and bring to a low boil.

Remove the mixture from the heat and stir in the chocolate. Let the syrup stand for about 30 seconds and stir until smooth. Cool before using and store, covered, in the refrigerator for up to 1 month.

caramel sauce

This recipe makes a thick syrup that becomes spreadable when cooled. It's as good warmed up and poured over ice cream as it is spread on cookies. For a slightly thinner caramel sauce, bring the initial temperature to 240°F.

ABOUT 2 CUPS SAUCE

¾ cup (6 ounces) heavy cream

6 tablespoons (¾ stick) unsalted butter, divided

½ teaspoon vanilla extract

½ teaspoon salt

1 cup (200 grams) muscavado or cane sugar

½ cup (4 ounces) brown rice syrup

In a heavy-bottomed pot over medium-low heat, warm the heavy cream and 3 tablespoons of the butter until the butter melts. Add the vanilla and salt, remove from the heat, and set aside.

In a separate heavy-bottomed pot, combine the sugar and brown rice syrup. Bring to a boil over medium heat, reduce the heat to medium low, and, without stirring, simmer until the mixture reaches 280°F. Remove the sugar mixture from the heat and carefully add the cream mixture to it. Exercise caution, as the mixture will bubble fiercely. Stir until the mixture is smooth. Place the pot back over medium heat and bring the mixture to 240°F, stirring occasionally. Stir in the remaining 3 tablespoons of butter. When the butter is entirely incorporated, remove the mixture from the heat. Allow the mixture to cool only slightly before transferring to a glass container for storage. Store in the refrigerator for up to 1 month. The sauce can be reheated in the microwave to soften when needed.

For an easy *vegan* Caramel Sauce, mix 1 cup rice milk with 1 tablespoon brown rice syrup, ½ cup of cane sugar, ¼ teaspoon arrowroot, and a pinch of salt in a heavy pot over medium-high heat, and bring to a boil. Reduce the temperature to low and, stirring occasionally, continue to cook for about 45 minutes or until the mixture becomes syrupy. It will thicken slightly as it cools.

snack cake crème

Like most commercial snack cake crème, this recipe contains no cream. Unlike a surprising amount of commercial snack cakes, however, this recipe does not contain beef suet. Health food? No. But a whole lot less gross than what you might find in many store-bought brands.

ABOUT 1 CUP CRÈME

2 tablespoons white spelt or ground millet flour

½ cup milk

½ cup (100 grams) cane sugar

½ teaspoon vanilla extract

4 tablespoons (½ stick) unsalted butter, cut into pieces

4 tablespoons coconut oil

Dash of salt (optional)

Combine the flour and milk in a saucepan over medium heat to form a thin, pale paste, about 4 to 5 minutes, stirring constantly. Be careful not to brown the roux. Stir in the sugar and continue to cook until smooth, about 2 to 3 minutes. Remove from the heat and stir in the vanilla. Cover and refrigerate to cool completely.

In the bowl of a stand mixer fitted with the whisk attachment, whisk the butter and coconut oil until light, about 1 minute. Add the cooled flour paste and beat until creamy, about 5 minutes. Store in an airtight container at room temperature for up to 2 days.

For gluten-free Snack Cake Crème, use the ground millet flour instead of the white spelt.

For vegan Snack Cake Crème, replace the milk with an equal amount of rice milk and the butter with an equal amount of coconut oil.

marshmallow crème

Here's a secret: Marshmallow crème is just seven-minute frosting. While this recipe probably makes more fluff than you need, don't be tempted to make a half recipe as two egg whites fluff better than one. Also, don't be tempted to replace the corn syrup with a less refined sugar; they simply won't work to create the marshmallowy texture.

ABOUT 3 CUPS CRÈME

½ cup (100 grams) plus 1 tablespoon cane sugar, divided

1 tablespoon corn syrup

1½ tablespoons water

2 egg whites

Pinch of cream of tartar

Combine ½ cup of the sugar, the corn syrup, and water in a heavy-bottomed pot and affix a candy thermometer to the side of the pot. Heat the mixture over medium heat, stirring continuously. Use a moistened pastry brush to brush down any errant crystals that form on the side of the pot. When the sugar has completely melted, stop stirring, but continue to cook until the mixture reaches 235°F.

While the sugar is cooking, combine the egg whites and cream of tartar in the bowl of a stand mixer fitted with the whisk attachment. Whisk until frothy. Gradually pour in the remaining 1 tablespoon of sugar and continue to beat until soft peaks form.

Once the sugar mixture reaches 235°F, add it to the egg white mixture: with the mixer on medium speed, very gradually stream the hot sugar syrup along the side of the bowl and into the egg whites. Beat until fluffy and shiny, 1 to 2 minutes. This crème will start to separate after about a day, so it is best used immediately.

> While there is no perfect vegan variation for Marshmallow Crème, you can use the Vegan Snack Cake Crème (page 140) as a substitute.

chocolate hazelnut spread

Although Nutella's chocolate hazelnut spread is free from artificial colors and preservatives, it's still fun (and easy) to make your own.

1½ CUPS SPREAD

- 1 cup (150 grams) raw hazelnuts
- 4 ounces dark chocolate, coarsely chopped
- 4 tablespoons (½ stick) unsalted butter, cut into ½-inch cubes
- ⅓ cup (35 grams) cocoa powder
- ½ teaspoon salt
- ¾ cup (100 grams) powdered sugar, divided

Preheat the oven to 400°F. Spread the hazelnuts on a baking sheet and toast them until the skins darken but don't burn. Let them cool for about 5 minutes and then rub them with a dish towel to remove the skins.

In the bowl of a food processor fitted with the metal blade, blend the hazelnuts until they are a smooth paste. This will take some patience. Scrape down the sides of the bowl several times during the process to keep the nuts blending; eventually they will start giving off oils and become smooth. This will take 5 to 10 minutes.

While the nuts are blending, bring a pot of water to a simmer. Place the chocolate and butter in a heatproof bowl over the simmering water and stir to melt. Add the cocoa powder and mix until there are no lumps. Pour the chocolate mixture into the bowl of the food processor with the hazelnut paste and blend. Add the salt and ¼ cup of the powdered sugar and blend. Taste the mixture and add additional powdered sugar to taste. The spread will thicken as it cools. Store in an airtight container in the refrigerator for up to 1 month. The spread can be reheated in the microwave to soften when needed.

For vegan Chocolate Hazelnut Spread, replace the butter with an equal amount of coconut oil.

white icing

This quick-to-make icing is great for adding a little ornamentation to your treats. It's smooth and pliable enough to write with and dries to a shiny, opaque white. For chocolate icing, add two teaspoons cocoa powder along with the other ingredients.

ABOUT ½ CUP ICING

2 tablespoons (¼ stick) unsalted butter

½ cup (65 grams) powdered sugar

1 teaspoon milk

1 teaspoon vanilla

Combine the butter, powdered sugar, milk, and vanilla in a medium bowl. With a hand mixer, beat until smooth. Use immediately.

> For vegan White Icing, replace the butter with an equal amount of coconut oil and the milk with an equal amount of soy or almond milk or water.

. . . .

glaze

This easy glaze is perfect for drizzling on Cinnamon Rolls (page 19) or spreading on Toaster Tarts (page 23), and you can substitute in your favorite flavors (maple, honey, orange) for the vanilla to create delicious variations.

ABOUT ½ CUP GLAZE

½ cup (65 grams) powdered sugar

2 teaspoons milk, divided

1 teaspoon vanilla extract

Sift the powdered sugar into a bowl and add the milk, one teaspoon at a time, mixing thoroughly with a spoon until a smooth paste forms. Stir in the vanilla. The mixture should drip when you hold up the spoon. Add a bit more milk if needed. Use immediately.

> For vegan Glaze, replace the milk with an equal amount of water or non-dairy milk.

sprinkles, jimmies, and dots

When you need a little extra something on your cupcakes or ice cream, these little sprinkles can add a little color. Replace the vanilla with other flavor extracts of your choice for something different.

ABOUT ½ CUP

1½ cups (200 grams) powdered sugar

½ teaspoons fine salt

1 egg white

1 teaspoon vanilla extract

Assorted natural food colorings

Line a baking sheet with parchment and set aside.

In a small bowl, mix the powdered sugar, salt, egg white, and vanilla to create a smooth paste. Divide the paste into small bowls for different colors and stir in the food coloring.

Spoon the paste into a piping bag fitted with a very small plain tip.

For sprinkles and jimmies, pipe tiny lines along the prepared baking sheet, leaving at least ½ inch of space between each line. Slice into your preferred size of jimmy or sprinkle and let dry at room temperature for 24 hours before using.

For dots, pipe tiny dots onto the prepared baking sheet, leaving at least ½ inch between dots. Let dry at room temperature for 24 hours before using. Store in an airtight container up to 1 month.

For vegan Sprinkles, Jimmies, and Dots, skip the egg and add 1 tablespoon of non-dairy milk instead. The sprinkles won't have quite the same shine, but they should still taste delicious.

yogurt coating

Use high-quality yogurt for this recipe, making sure to avoid those that are made with gelatin. If you use thick Greek-style yogurt, there's no need to strain it first. To help the yogurt coating set, this recipe uses agar powder, which can be found in Asian markets. Look for Telephone brand, which doesn't have the chemical odors that some agar powder has. The coating is best used immediately, so plan accordingly.

ABOUT 1½ CUPS COATING

¼ cup (2 ounces) plain whole milk yogurt

1 tablespoon cane sugar

¼ teaspoon agar powder

1 teaspoon water

1¾ cups (240 grams) powdered sugar

1 teaspoon brown rice syrup or golden syrup

Pinch of salt

1 teaspoon vanilla extract

Line a colander with cheesecloth and place it over a bowl. Place the yogurt in the colander and pull the cheesecloth up around it. Refrigerate and let drain at least 2 hours, or overnight. Discard the liquid that accumulates in the bowl.

Mix the cane sugar and agar powder with the water and microwave for 30 seconds on full power. Set aside.

Combine the powdered sugar, brown rice syrup, salt, vanilla, and yogurt solids in the bowl of a stand mixer fitted with the paddle attachment and mix on medium speed until smooth and creamy, 1 to 2 minutes. If the mixture is too thick, add a bit of unstrained yogurt and blend again to combine. Pour in the agar syrup, and mix until smooth, scraping down the sides of the bowl as needed.

Use the mixture immediately to dip your snacks, and dry them on waxed paper or on a wire rack to set for about 30 minutes.

To reuse any leftover coating that has set, heat it on low power in the microwave until it loosens and then proceed as if it were fresh.

For vegan Yogurt Coating, replace the yogurt with an equal amount of vanilla non-dairy yogurt and omit the vanilla extract.

vanilla extract

It's amazing to me that we pay twelve dollars or more for an ounce or two of high-quality flavor extracts when they are so easy to make at home. All you need are some bottles, a high-proof alcohol, and whatever flavor you want to create.

1 PINT EXTRACT

3 to 5 vanilla beans

1 pint vodka or white rum

Score the vanilla beans down the middle and place them in a tall bottle with a tightly fitting cap. Fill with vodka. Place in a dark cabinet for at least 2 weeks. Top off with more of the alcohol after each use. Every 6 months or so, replace the vanilla beans with new ones. The extract will keep indefinitely in a dark cabinet.

mint extract

The flavor of your Mint Extract depends greatly on the flavor of the mint leaves you use. Personally, I like chocolate mint leaf, since most of my Mint Extract goes into chocolate treats. If you want your extract to be green, add a drop or two of food coloring. Store-bought mint extract is far more potent than this home version, so you'll need to add to taste when using it in recipes.

8 OUNCES EXTRACT

½ cup mint leaves, washed and dried

8 ounces vodka

Bruise the mint leaves slightly. Place them in an 8-ounce bottle with a tightly fitting cap. Pour in the vodka. Place in a dark cabinet for at least 2 weeks. Strain the mixture through cheesecloth, discarding the leaves. Store the extract in the refrigerator for up to 2 months.

cooking spray

I love to use oil sprays to coat baking pans or to give just a little spritz of oil to a salad or chip. But I hate using aerosol cans. Here's a great alternative. Use any oil you'd like.

Oil

Pump spray bottle

Pour the oil into the pump spray bottle. The resulting oil mist may not be quite as fine as that from an aerosol can, but it will meet most of your baking spray needs. Store indefinitely in a dark cabinet.

. . . .

onion or garlic powder

While a food dehydrator will do a better job of preserving the pale color of onions and garlic, your oven on its lowest temperature will do the job and create dried slices that are easily pulverized into a sweet, caramel-colored powder. For a fragrant salt, mix one part powder with two parts fine salt. You can also use this method to create shallot, chile, or bell pepper powder.

ABOUT ½ CUP POWDER

½ pound onion or garlic, peeled and thinly sliced

Place the onion or garlic slices on the tray of a food dehydrator and dehydrate for 6 to 8 hours until the slices are completely dry. Use a spice grinder to mill into a fine powder.

If you do not have a food dehydrator, preheat the oven to 150°F. Line a baking sheet with foil. Spread the onion or garlic slices evenly over the prepared baking sheet and bake until dry, about 3 hours. Cool to room temperature and use a spice grinder to mill into a fine powder. Store in an airtight container up to 1 month.

sour cream and onion flavoring

Feel free to get as oniony (or not) as you'd like with this homemade sour cream and onion flavor. I love the little specks of green that dried chives give, but onion powder will give you more flavoring.

ABOUT ⅛ CUP FLAVORING

1½ teaspoons sea salt

6 teaspoons Sour Cream Powder (page 154) or powdered buttermilk

1 teaspoon Onion Powder (page 149) or finely chopped dried chives

Combine the sea salt, sour cream powder, and onion powder in an airtight container. Store the powder in an airtight container in the refrigerator for up to 2 weeks, or in the freezer for up to 1 month.

For **vegan** Sour Cream and Onion Flavoring, replace the Sour Cream Powder with powdered Vegan Cashew Cream (page 154).

bbq flavoring

This chip (or cracker) seasoning is a great blend of smoky, salty, and sweet.

ABOUT ⅛ CUP FLAVORING

3 teaspoons smoked paprika

3 teaspoons garlic salt

1½ teaspoons sugar

1½ teaspoons Onion Powder (page 149)

1½ teaspoons chili powder

1 teaspoon ground mustard

Dash of cayenne pepper

Combine the paprika, garlic salt, sugar, onion powder, chili powder, ground mustard, and cayenne pepper in an airtight container. Mixture will keep for up to 1 month at room temperature.

ranch flavoring

While this recipe makes just enough flavoring for a single recipe of chips or crackers, it stores well, so feel free to make a much larger batch to have on hand to sprinkle on popcorn or even a baked potato.

ABOUT ⅛ CUP FLAVORING

1 teaspoon Onion Powder (page 149)

1 teaspoon Garlic Powder (page 149)

1 teaspoon dried cilantro

1 teaspoon dried dill

6 teaspoons Sour Cream Powder (page 154) or powdered buttermilk

1 teaspoon salt

Pinch of cayenne pepper

Combine the onion powder, garlic powder, cilantro, dill, Sour Cream Powder, salt, and cayenne pepper. Store the powder in an airtight container in the refrigerator for up to 2 weeks, or in the freezer for up to 1 month.

For vegan Ranch Flavoring, replace the Sour Cream Powder with powdered Vegan Cashew Cream (page 154).

cheese powder

I learned this trick of turning almost any cheese into a powder from Seattle Food Geek's Scott Heimendinger (SeattleFoodGeek.com), whose DIY molecular gastronomy is always as entertaining as it is informative. Scott makes his own tapioca granules by grinding up small pearl tapioca in a spice grinder, but starting with tapioca starch is a bit quicker and makes a lighter, fluffier cheese powder. I use cheddar here, but you can use any favorite cheese. Have fun!

ABOUT ½ CUP POWDER

2 ounces grated cheddar cheese

1 teaspoon water

¼ to ⅓ cup (35 to 60 grams) tapioca starch

½ teaspoon salt

¼ teaspoon sugar

Preheat the oven to its lowest setting, 170°F to 200°F. Line a baking sheet with parchment or a silicone baking mat and set aside.

Combine the cheese and water in a small saucepan over medium-low heat, stirring until the cheese has melted. Stir constantly so the cheese doesn't brown.

Combine the melted cheese and 35 grams of the tapioca starch in the bowl of a food processor fitted with the metal blade. Pulse until the mixture resembles breadcrumbs. If the mixture begins to resemble dough, add a bit more tapioca starch, and pulse again. Continue to add tapioca starch until the crumbs feel dry to the touch.

Spread the cheese crumbs evenly on the prepared baking sheet and bake until the cheese crumbs are completely dry, about 45 minutes. Cool for 10 minutes. Pulse in a spice grinder or blender, along with the salt and sugar, until the mixture is a fine powder. If the mixture is too moist, add another 10 to 20 grams of tapioca starch. Store the cheese powder in an airtight container in the refrigerator for up to 2 weeks, or in the freezer for up to 1 month.

While there is no perfect vegan variation for this powder, you can use nutritional yeast or powdered Vegan Cashew Cream (page 154) as a substitution.

sour cream powder

Dehydrated sour cream is a great addition to any chip seasoning. Follow this same process to make powdered yogurt, which is great anywhere you'd use powdered sour cream.

ABOUT ⅓ CUP POWDER

½ cup sour cream

Spread the sour cream very thinly with an offset spatula over strips of parchment. Place the strips on the tray of a food dehydrator and dehydrate until the sour cream becomes mostly transparent and fully dry, about 5 hours.

If you do not have a food dehydrator, preheat the oven to 150°F (or as low as your oven will go). Line a baking sheet with parchment. Spread the sour cream very thinly with an offset spatula over the parchment. If your oven has a fan, turn it on, and cook until the sour cream is completely dry, 4 to 5 hours.

Scrape the dried sour cream off the parchment (it should easily release) and into a food processor, blender, or spice grinder. Blend to a fine powder. Store in an airtight container in the refrigerator for up to 2 weeks, or in the freezer for up to 1 month.

vegan cashew cream

This cream is a great substitution whenever you need sour cream, and can be dehydrated as a great vegan variation for the Sour Cream Powder.

ABOUT ½ CUP CREAM
OR ⅓ CUP POWDER

¼ cup raw cashews

½ tablespoon lemon juice

½ teaspoon apple cider vinegar

Salt

¼ to ⅓ cup water

Soak the cashews in water for 1 to 2 hours.

Drain the cashews, then blend with the lemon juice, vinegar, a pinch of salt, and the water until creamy and smooth.

For powdered Vegan Cashew Cream, dehydrate the cream by following the Sour Cream Powder instructions above.

INDEX

ABOUT THE AUTHOR

lara ferroni is a former tech geek turned food geek who spends her days exploring the food culture of the Pacific Northwest. As a writer and photographer, she might be spotted digging through bargain bins for the perfect prop, dreaming up delicious new ways to use teff, or eating and drinking her way through Portland's vibrant food scene. Her photos have been featured on Gourmet.com, Epicurious.com, *Imbibe* and *Edible Communities* magazines, as well as over ten cookbooks, including her own, *Doughnuts*. You can find more of her tasty photos and recipes at LaraFerroni.com.